sensations

Editor: Lydia Leong
Designer: Lynn Chin Nyuk Ling
Photographer: Edmond Ho

Copyright © 2007 Marshall Cavendish International (Asia) Private Limited
Case with jacket edition 2007
This paperback edition 2011

Published by Marshall Cavendish Cuisine
An imprint of Marshall Cavendish International
1 New Industrial road, Singapore 536196

Other Marshall Cavendish Offices:

Marshall Cavendish International. PO Box 65829 London EC1P 1NY, UK • Marshall Cavendish Corporation.
99 White Plains Road, Tarrytown NY 10591-9001, USA • Marshall Cavendish International (Thailand) Co Ltd.
253 Asoke, 12th Flr, Sukhumvit 21 Road, Klongtoey Nua, Wattana, Bangkok 10110, Thailand • Marshall
Cavendish (Malaysia) Sdn Bhd, Times Subang, Lot 46, Subang Hi-Tech Industrial Park, Batu Tiga, 40000
Shah Alam, Selangor Darul Ehsan, Malaysia

Marshall Cavendish is a trademark of Times Publishing Limited

National Library Board, Singapore Cataloguing-in-Publication Data

Leong, Sam, 1966-
Sensations : a tasting menu of Chinese-inspired flavours / Sam Leong. – Singapore : Marshall Cavendish Cuisine,
2011, c2007.
p. cm.
ISBN : 978-981-4351-12-6 (pbk.)

1. Cooking, Chinese. I. Title.

TX724.5.C5
641.5951 -- dc22   OCN706348926

Printed in Singapore by KWF Printing Pte Ltd

sensations

A TASTING MENU OF CHINESE-INSPIRED FLAVOURS

Sam Leong

mc Marshall Cavendish
Cuisine

Dedication

To my mum and dad who made me what I am today.

献给我亲爱的父母：感谢您对我辛勤的培养！

Acknowledgements

This book, the concept and recipes, has been on my mind for several years, and it is now ready, like a dish, fragrant and pipping hot from the wok, for all to enjoy. But it would not have been possible without the many people who have supported me through the years.

I would like to thank:

my wife, Forest Leong, for being my constant companion. I would also like to commend and congratulate her for using her culinary skills to start a private kitchen in our home.

my sons, Leong Yew Choong and Leong Yew Jhow, for their maturity in bearing with my long hours at work.

my mother, for never giving up on me. I am glad I am now someone she can be proud of.

Andrew Tjioe for giving me endless opportunities to advance my career.

the front service and kitchen staff of the Tung Lok Group for being the backbone of the restaurant operations.

Peter Knipp, for opening the doors for me into the Singapore food scene and for being my mentor.

Mr Yap Kim Wah, Ms Betty Wong, Mr Hermann and the management and staff of SIA, for guiding me and giving me the opportunity to become part of the International Culinary Panel (ICP).

Debe Ho, for giving me the opportunity to do my first television programme, *King of Kitchens*.

the management and staff of MediaCorp TV for inviting me to be the chef-mentor for *Star Chefs*.

my supporters and guests, for enjoying my culinary creations these 15 years.

the media, for their enthusiasm about my cuisine.

Marshall Cavendish International (Asia) Pte Ltd, especially David Yip, for another opportunity to fulfil my dream.

Lydia Leong, for helping me refine my thoughts and putting them into words.

Lynn Chin, for her creativity in putting the design of this book together.

Edmond Ho, for making my dishes come alive through his lenses.

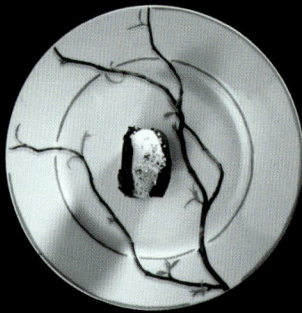

Contents

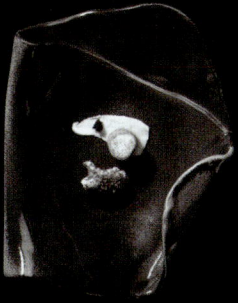

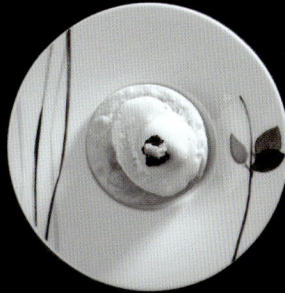

Foreword

Chef Sam Leong's cuisine is both brilliant and electrifying. His ability to interpret and influence traditional Chinese food using modern techniques and sensibilities showcases his intimate understanding of this age-old cuisine. The presentation, also an art form, is very much similar to the Japanese kaiseki meal, where the season's best offerings are artfully arranged and presented.

This nouveau approach to Chinese cuisine makes manifest Sam's passion and expression through his cutting edge ideas, creative recipes and precision execution. These recipes capture the essence of the incredible flavour structure of the dishes in every bite.

Sam has tremendous talent and an incredible gift of cooking and teaching. With these abilities, he provides us with the magical opportunity to understand and enjoy all his signature dishes without diminishing their complexities or sophistication. He raises the bar on passionate Chinese cooking, and encourages us to take notice of this remarkable cuisine and understand how it should be enjoyed.

As you enter this exciting journey through Sam's mind of exotic Asia, you realise how much restraint and discipline he uses in order to highlight the ingredients, their taste and flavours in each carefully crafted dish. His refinement and elegance rival those of any three-star French kitchen across the globe.

A well-respected authority of modern Chinese and Singapore cooking, Sam has, with this book, taken us to a new level of excellence. *Sensations: A Tasting Menu of Chinese-inspired Flavours* provides us all with continued excitement and even greater pleasure in modern Chinese cuisine.

Lee Hefter
Executive Chef and Managing Partner
Spago Beverly Hills and
Wolfgang Puck Fine Dining Group

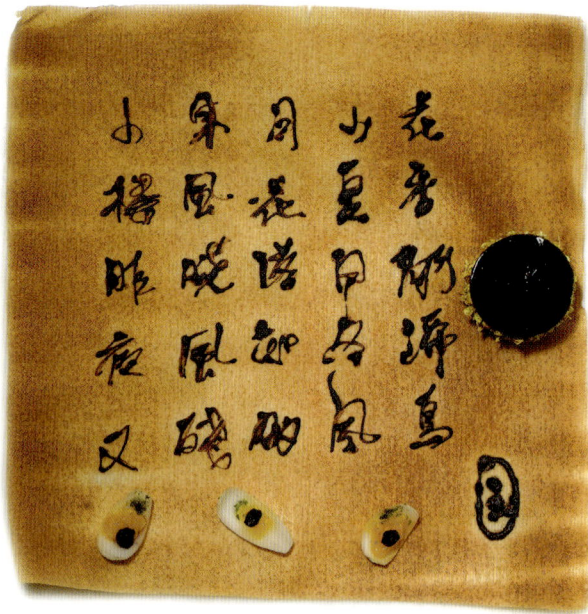

Introduction

The Inspiration

I trained as a chef in Cantonese cooking under my father, Leong Mun Soon, who was known as the King of Shark's Fin back in the 1960s in Malaysia. Under his tutelage, I built a strong foundation in the traditional methods of cooking. It was not until I was in my early 20s that I started travelling and learnt more about European cuisine. I noticed the differences from the cuisine that I had grown to know and love so well. Food was plated and served in individual portions, and exciting ingredients such as caviar, truffle and foie gras were used. Inspired, I took these observations home with me and came up with a new type of Chinese cuisine. Although it was difficult to introduce a modern interpretation to a traditional cuisine, I persevered and soon the cuisine gained acceptance and has now been termed modern Chinese cuisine. Today, many Chinese restaurants in Singapore have started serving modern Chinese cuisine.

I am happy that modern Chinese cuisine has come to be widely accepted and practised. And I know that Chinese cuisine can be taken to yet another level. My travels to Japan and France led me to think about the Japanese concept of kaiseki and the French dégustation menu. Kaiseki is an elegant meal served during the Japanese tea ceremony. There can be as many as eight to 32 courses, each served in delicate portions and beautifully presented not only to excite the taste buds, but also to seduce the diner visually. A menu dégustation is also served in small portions to allow the diner to sample all of the chef's signature dishes in one sitting. Could these concepts be combined with modern Chinese cuisine, where a guest is served a minimum of eight courses and up to a maximum of 24 courses?

The Senses of Sight, Smell, Taste and Touch

This book showcases my initial foray into modern Chinese fine dining, where modern Chinese cuisine is crafted and plated in small portions not only to excite the palate and eyes, but to allow the diner to indulge his whole being in the dining experience and be seduced by his senses.

It is my hope that the cooking techniques, food presentation, style and design of this book will rekindle interest in Chinese cooking and inspire young, upcoming chefs to explore Chinese cuisine, and to approach it with a fresh perspective.

The recipes included in this book are meant to be prepared and served freely, without restriction, according to your guests' preferences. That is, prepare and serve more soups if a lighter meal is preferred, or more meat dishes if desired. There is no rule or order to keep to. Just be aware of what your guests prefer and use that as your guide.

Sam Leong

Appetisers

COMBINATION of SEARED
SCALLOP on
PINEAPPLE and CRISPY
PRAWN on WATERMELON
recipe p129

遠上寒山石徑斜

白雲深處有人家

停車坐愛楓林晚

BEIJING-STYLE CUCUMBER SALAD
IN HOMEMADE VINAIGRETTE
recipe p130

CHILLED ROASTED AUBERGINE JELLY
WITH WOLFBERRIES AND BABY CLAMS

recipe p131

BEEF CARPACCIO WITH SAUTÉED BARLEY IN YUZU JELLY

recipe p132

WOK-FRIED GLUTEN WITH
GINGKO NUTS AND **MUSHROOMS**
recipe p133

CRISPY CHICKEN FLOSS ROLL COATED WITH SESAME SEEDS AND TOPPED WITH TOMATO SALSA

recipe p134

W A F E R P A P E R

Wafer paper is a starch-based confection that melts away when cooked. This edible paper serves to hold ingredients together while they are being cooked, then dissolves without a trace. It is commonly used as a food wrapper for deep-frying, such as with fried ice cream.

CRISPY CRABMEAT PASTRY WITH FOIE GRAS BRAISED IN SOY SAUCE

recipe p135

CRABMEAT AND SWEET BLACK PLUM TOSSED WITH SOUR PLUM DRESSING IN CHERRY TOMATO

recipe p136

SEA CUCUMBER ON JULIENNE SNOW PEAS
recipe p137

BANANA SEA CUCUMBERS

Banana sea cucumbers are small, measuring about 8 cm (3 in) in length, less than half the size of the more common sea cucumber, which can grow up to 20 cm (8 in). Both dried and reconstituted sea cucumbers are available from the markets and supermarkets. Reconstituted ones are convenient to use. Sea cucumbers are considered a delicacy and are often served during the Chinese new year period. After cooking, banana sea cucumbers are tender and chewy.

CHILLED LOBSTER
WITH **THREE DRESSINGS**
recipe p138

FRESH SHARK'S FIN
IN XO SAUCE

recipe p139

CHAWANMUSHI WITH
BLACK TRUFFLE SAUCE AND
CRISPY CHEESE CRACKER
recipe p140

S O Y   B E A N   C R U M B

A product from Taiwan, soy bean crumb is made
of soy beans that are dry-roasted and chopped,
then compressed into a ball.

TEMPURA OYSTER COATED
WITH **LEMON CITRUS CREAM** AND
CRISPY SOY BEAN CRUMB
recipe p141

WHITE ASPARAGUS
WITH CRABMEAT
IN GINGER DRESSING
recipe p142

STEAMED CRAB
CLAW with YUNNAN HAM
and GINGER
recipe p143

Soups

DOUBLE-BOILED PRAWN
DUMPLING IN HOT AND SOUR CONSOMMÉ

recipe p144

W A T E R   C H E S T N U T S

Water chestnuts grow in the marshes and may still have some mud on them when purchased at the markets or supermarkets. Rinse them well, then cut off the tops and peel off the skin before use. The white flesh is sweet and crunchy and can be eaten raw, or chopped and boiled with rock sugar for a cooling drink. Canned water chestnuts may be used if fresh water chestnuts are not available. Water chestnuts are used in both sweet and savoury preparations in Chinese cooking.

STEAMED CRAB CLAW WITH BAMBOO PITHS AND CORDYCEPS IN SUPERIOR CHICKEN CONSOMMÉ

recipe p145

WILD   BAMBOO   PITH

Wild bamboo piths are highly prized, as they are crunchier and have a firmer texture compared to farmed bamboo piths. Bamboo piths are commonly used in Chinese cooking to add bite to stir-fries and braised dishes. Bamboo piths are sold dried and need to be soaked in several changes of water until the water is clear. Drain and squeeze out any excess water before adding the piths to the pot.

SHARK'S FIN WITH ALASKAN
CRABMEAT IN EGG WHITE SAUCE
recipe p147

JULIENNE CHICKEN, SNOW PEAS, YUNNAN HAM AND DRIED SCALLOPS IN SUPERIOR BROTH

recipe p148

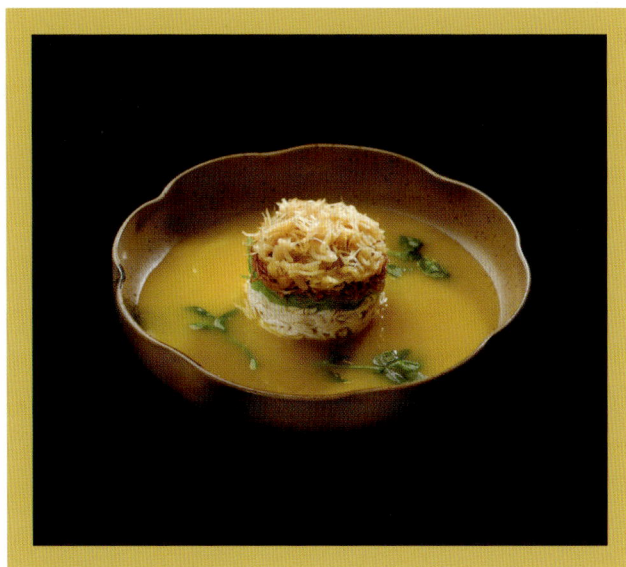

CHILLED MOREL CONSOMMÉ

recipe p149

C H I N E S E   W O L F B E R R I E S

Chinese wolfberries play an important role in Traditional Chinese Medicine (TCM) where the small red berries are believed to improve vision and promote the body's blood circulation among other beneficial effects. Sold dried, Chinese wolfberries are sweet and can be eaten raw or cooked, just as with raisins.

Fish and Seafood

STEAMED AUSTRALIAN LOBSTER WITH FRESH AND FRIED GARLIC IN FLAVOURED SAUCE

recipe p150

WOK-FRIED BAMBOO CLAMS
WITH BLACK BEANS AND ROASTED GARLIC
recipe p151

LYCHEES

Lychees have a rough textured skin that is deep red in colour. The skin can be easily peeled off to reveal thick, juicy, translucent white flesh. Canned lychees make good substitutes if fresh ones are not available. A superior type of lychee is the *lor mai chi*. Its thick, succulent flesh is very sweet and the fruit has only a very small seed.

TEMPURA LYCHEE STUFFED WITH CURRIED CRABMEAT

recipe p152

SEARED SCALLOP STUFFED
WITH PEAR IN WARM MANGO SAUCE
recipe p153

CRISPY PAN-SEARED CRABMEAT DUMPLING

recipe p154

SCRAMBLED EGG WITH SHARK'S FIN AND CRABMEAT

recipe p155

WOK-FRIED CRABMEAT
AND ROE WITH EGG WHITE
recipe p156

CRISPY MARBLE GOBY
WITH MANGO AND SWEET CHILLI SAUCE

recipe p157

STEAMED YABBY DUMPLING

recipe p158

PINK PEPPERCORNS

Pink peppercorns are not part of the pepper family. They are the dried fruit of the Baies Rose and are treasured for their sweet peppery flavour. Pink peppercorns are popularly used in French cooking and to flavour oils. Crush the pink peppercorns between your thumb and forefinger to release their full flavour before using.

TRADITIONAL AND MODERN SIEW MAI
recipe p159

SPARAGUS, BLACK TRUFFLE AND ENOKI MUSHROOM
recipe p160

BAKED COD FILLET WITH
SCRAMBLED EGG WHITE

recipe p161

WOK-FRIED LOBSTER WITH SALTED EGG YOLK

recipe p162

CRISPY FISH FILLET WITH SPICY FRISÉE SALAD

recipe p163

FROG LEG WITH CRISPY
SOY BEAN CRUMB AND ANGLED LUFFA

recipe p164

DEEP-FRIED AND STEAMED
FISH HEAD WITH PICKLED RED CHILLIES
AND SALTED BLACK BEANS

recipe p165

RED CHILLIES

Red chillies are often used to add spice and colour to dishes. There are over 200 kinds of chillies, ranging from yellow, to green and red, and even black. The size of chillies offers a basic indication of their spiciness—large chillies are often mild, while small ones are often the hottest.

Meat and Poultry

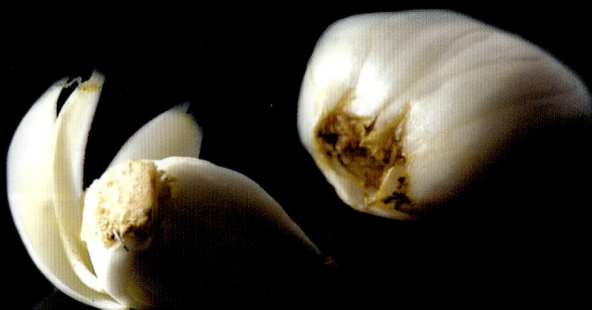

FRESH LILY BULBS

Fresh lily bulbs (*bai he*) are creamy white in colour and resemble peeled garlic bulbs. They have a sweet, mild flavour and are used in Traditional Chinese Medicine (TCM) for remedies to the heart and lung. Sauté lightly with green leafy vegetables to enjoy the simple goodness of fresh lily bulbs.

COFFEE BEEF TENDERLOIN
WITH SAUTÉED FRESH LILY BULBS
recipe p166

ROAST SUCKLING PIG SKIN WITH
SEARED FOIE GRAS AND CHEESE CRACKER

recipe p167

STEAMED LION'S HEAD

recipe p168

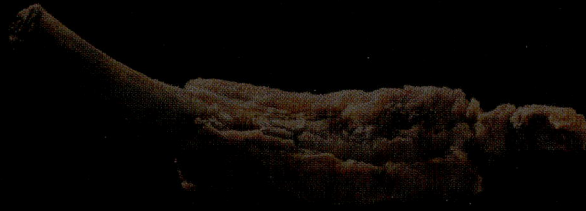

BRAISED PORK RIB IN SWEET AND SOUR SAUCE

recipe p169

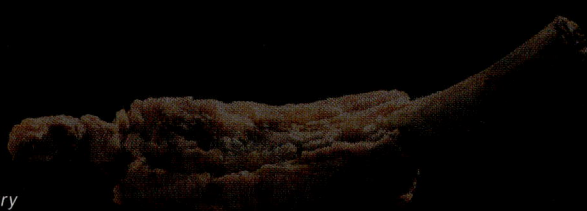

ROSELLA FLOWERS

Part of the hibiscus family, rosella flowers are commonly used in Thai cooking and in the preparation of jams and beverages. A sauce made from the rosella flower is often served with foie gras in modern Chinese restaurants.

SEARED FOIE GRAS with CARAMELISED APPLE

recipe p170

SEARED FOIE GRAS WITH CARAMELISED STRAWBERRY AND PEKING DUCK SKIN WITH CURRY-MAYO PRAWN

recipe p171

SEARED WAGYU BEEF WITH ASSORTED
SALAD GREENS IN CRISPY CHEESE BASKET

recipe p172

SHANGHAINESE
GLASS NOODLES
WITH ROASTED
LEMON GRASS CHICKEN

recipe p173

SEARED DUCK BREAST AND FOIE GRAS
WITH SAUTÉED POTATOES IN HOISIN SAUCE

recipe p174

BRAISED OX TAIL WITH RADISH

recipe p175

Vegetables and Mushrooms

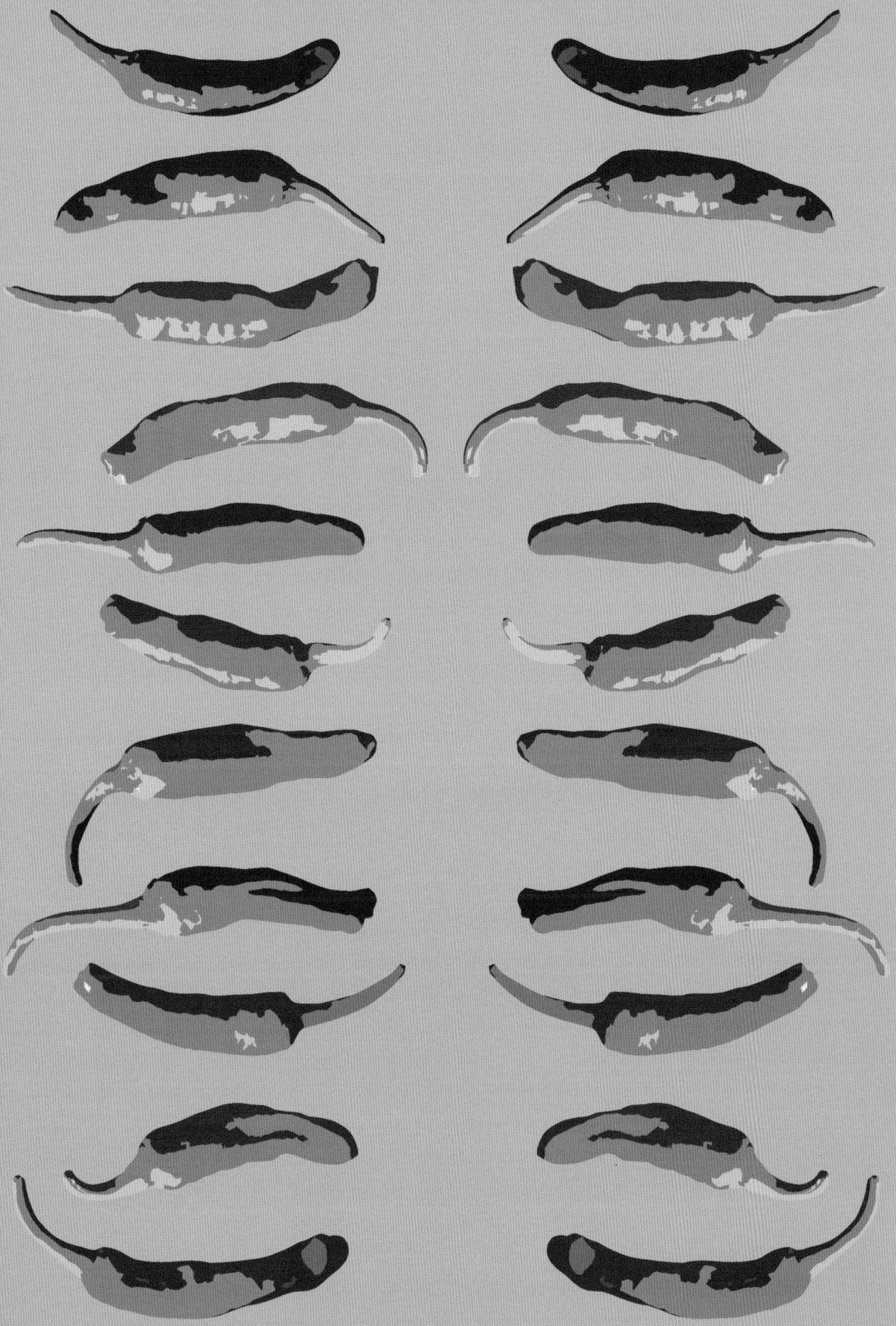

DEEP-FRIED BEAN CURD, PRAWN AND
SPINACH BALL COATED WITH BREAD CUBES
recipe p177

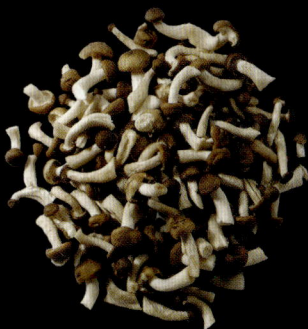

Hon shimeji mushrooms grow in compact bunches with cream-coloured stems and may sport cream or brown caps. They have a nutty flavour and are commonly used in stir-fries or in stews and soups. To prepare these mushrooms, cut off the hard base and brush lightly to remove any dirt before cooking.

STEAMED ASSORTED MUSHROOMS
IN MUI CHOY LEAVES

recipe p122

SHISHITO PEPPERS

Shishito peppers are also known as Japanese chillies. They have a mild, sweet taste and a crunchy texture. They are commonly used in tempura and yakatori dishes, and are high in vitamins.

SICHUAN-STYLE WOK-FRIED
SHISHITO PEPPER WITH DRIED PRAWNS

recipe p179

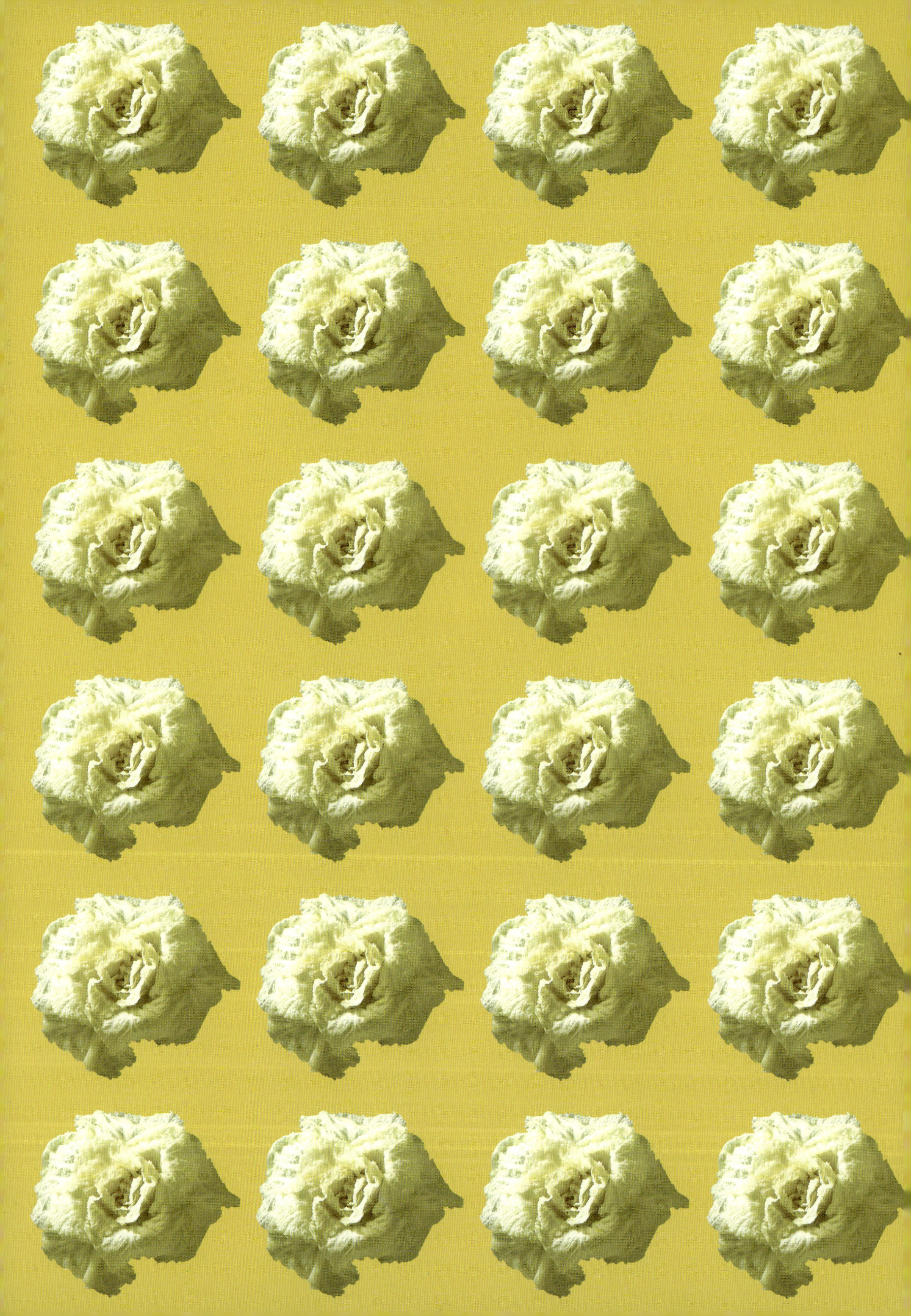

POACHED CHINESE CABBAGE WITH SALTED EGG CREAM SAUCE

recipe p180

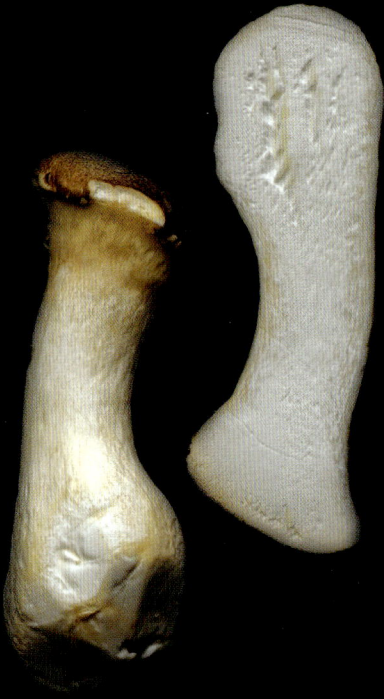

M U S H R O O M S

There are many varieties of mushrooms and they vary in shape, size, texture and colour. Mushrooms are rich in protein and are often used as a meat substitute in vegetarian cooking. When selecting fresh mushrooms, choose those that are firm and blemish-free. Use a dry brush or paper towel to clean off any dirt when preparing fresh mushrooms. Avoid washing them, as the flavour of the mushrooms will be lost.

PAN-SEARED WHOLE MUSHROOM WITH ASSORTED GREENS AND WALNUT DRESSING

recipe p181

Rice and Noodles

BRAISED MEE POK
WITH CLAMS AND
WHITE HON SHIMEJI
MUSHROOMS IN XO SAUCE
recipe p182

LA MIAN AND SEARED SRI LANKAN CRAB
CLAW IN SUPERIOR CHICKEN CONSOMMÉ
recipe p183

WARM GLUTINOUS RICE WITH LOTUS SEEDS ON ORANGE JUICE-MARINATED LOTUS ROOT SLICE

recipe p184

L O T U S   R O O T

This fibrous and starchy Asian root vegetable grows in the water. Its distinctive feature is the beautiful pattern of air holes that run through the centre of the root. Lotus root is sweet with a crunchy texture and can be used in soups, stir-fries and salads, or braised and steamed.

CHILLED LA MIAN
recipe p185

CLAMS

Clams have a tender and chewy texture, and are often served steamed, or in stir-fries and stews. Clams can be shucked or cooked in their shells. If cooking with the shells, scrub first to remove any algae or dirt. Dispose of any shells that do not open while cooking, as they are probably bad.

CRISPY EGG NOODLES
AND LARGE CLAMS
IN CHICKEN CONSOMMÉ

recipe p186

109

BAKED RICE WITH CRABMEAT AND CHEESE
recipe p187

BRAISED BEEF CONSOMMÉ LA MIAN

recipe p188

WARM GLUTINOUS RICE WITH SEARED FOIE GRAS

recipe p189

FRIED RICE WITH CRABMEAT, DRIED SCALLOPS, EGG WHITE AND BRAISED WHOLE ABALONE

recipe p190

Desserts

CHILLED PEAR with RED and WHITE WINE
recipe p191

WARM CHOCOLATE SOUFFLÉ
WITH BERRIES AND VANILLA ICE CREAM
recipe p192

YELLOW PUMPKIN CUSTARD

recipe p193

YELLOW PUMPKIN

Pumpkins are also known as squash. There are many varieties of pumpkin and they come in a range of sizes and colours. Pumpkins are used in both sweet and savoury preparations. The large, flat pumpkin seeds inside the pumpkin are often discarded, but they may be roasted for a tasty and nutritious snack.

MODERN TEOCHEW YAM PASTE

recipe p194

HOMEMADE LYCHEE SHERBET
recipe p195

Osmanthus blossoms (*gui hua*) are small, yellow flowers with a delightful sweet fragrance. The blossoms are dried and used in teas or desserts to add colour and fragrance.

STUFFED RED DATE
recipe p125

COCONUT ICE CREAM
ON YELLOW PUMPKIN PURÉE

recipe p197

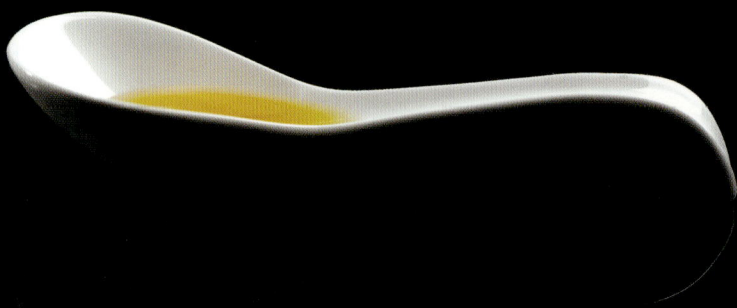

RECIPES

Appetisers

COMBINATION OF SEARED SCALLOP ON PINEAPPLE AND CRISPY PRAWN ON WATERMELON

SERVES 4

Scallop on Pineapple
Chicken consommé (see p133)
200 ml (6¹/₂ fl oz)

Honey ¹/₂ tsp

Tamarind pulp ¹/₂ tsp

Tomato sauce ¹/₂ tsp

Tabasco sauce 2–3 drops

Raisins 10

Pineapple cubes 4, each about
4-cm (1¹/₂-in)

Cooking oil 1 Tbsp

Scallops 4

Salt ¹/₄ tsp

Ground black pepper ¹/₄ tsp

Prawn on Watermelon
Prawns (shrimps) 4, peeled

Salt ¹/₈ tsp

Cornflour (cornstarch) 1 Tbsp

Cooking oil for deep-frying

Red watermelon cubes 4, each
about 4-cm (1¹/₂-in)

Sauce
Mayonnaise 6 tsp

Sweetened condensed milk 3 tsp

Seafood curry powder 1 tsp

Lemon juice 1 tsp

Garnish
Black ebiko

Chopped chives

Crispy soy bean crumb (see p141)
or fried minced garlic

Prepare the scallops on pineapple. Place the chicken consommé, honey, tamarind pulp, tomato sauce, Tabasco sauce, raisins and pineapple cubes in a small pot and simmer over low heat for about 30 minutes, or until all the liquid in the pot has completely evaporated. Set the pineapple cubes aside.

Heat the oil in a wok and sear the scallops. Season with salt and pepper, then place the scallops on the pineapple cubes. Garnish with black ebiko and chopped chives before serving.

Season the prawns with salt, then dust with cornflour. Heat the oil for deep-frying, then fry the prawns until crisp and golden brown. Remove the prawns and drain well.

Combine the ingredients for the sauce and toss with the fried prawns.

Place the deep-fried coated prawns on the watermelon cubes and garnish with the crispy soy bean crumb or fried minced garlic, and chives. Serve the combination of scallop on pineapple and prawn on watermelon immediately.

129

BEIJING-STYLE CUCUMBER SALAD IN HOMEMADE VINAIGRETTE

SERVES 4

Cooking oil *for deep-frying*
Tiger prawns (shrimps) *4*
Cornflour (cornstarch) *¹/₄ tsp*
Salt *¹/₄ tsp*
Japanese cucumber *1*

Homemade Vinaigrette
Black vinegar *100 ml (3¹/₃ fl oz)*
Honey *3 Tbsp*
Light soy sauce *20 ml (²/₃ fl oz)*
Dark soy sauce *¹/₄ tsp*

Garnish
Black caviar

Heat the oil for deep-frying in a wok.

Remove the heads of the prawns, then peel the shells off. Sprinkle the shelled heads with cornflour and salt, then deep-fry them until golden brown and crisp. Set the heads aside to drain well.

Bring a pot of water to the boil. Blanch the bodies of the prawns in the boiling water, then remove and plunge into another pot of cold water. Drain and shell, leaving the tails intact.

Combine all the ingredients for the homemade vinaigrette and mix well.

Peel and slice the cucumber into rounds, each about 1-cm (¹/₂-in) thick. Arrange each prawn on a cucumber round, top with a head and drizzle with vinaigrette. Garnish with caviar and serve immediately.

CHILLED ROASTED AUBERGINE JELLY WITH WOLFBERRIES AND BABY CLAMS

SERVES 4

Long aubergines (eggplants/brinjals)
  200 g (7 oz)

Salt *to taste*

Chicken consommé (see p133)
  100 ml (3¹/₃ fl oz)

Sweet mirin *3 tsp*

Sake *3 tsp*

Bonito flakes *20 g (²/₃ oz)*

Gelatine *1 sheet, soaked in cold water
  for 10 minutes*

Chinese wolfberries *30 g (1 oz),
  soaked for 30 minutes, then drained*

Baby clam meat *85 g (3 oz)*

Cooking oil *1 Tbsp*

Sugar *¼ tsp*

Oyster sauce *½ tsp*

Chinese cooking wine (*hua tiao*)
  ¹/₄ tsp

Cornflour (cornstarch) *¹/₄ tsp, mixed
  with ¹/₂ tsp water*

Garnish
Lemon or orange zest

Trim the ends of the aubergines, then cut the aubergines lengthwise in half. Sprinkle them with salt and place on a baking tray. Bake the aubergines in a preheated oven at 100°C (212°F) for 15 minutes, or until lightly charred and shrunken. Leave the aubergines to cool, then using a pair of chopsticks, pull the flesh from the skin. Discard the skin and set the flesh aside.

Combine the chicken consommé, mirin and sake in a small saucepan and bring to the boil. When the mixture comes to a boil, remove it from the heat and add the bonito flakes. Cover the saucepan and leave it for about 15 minutes. Strain the mixture and discard the bonito flakes. Reheat the mixture over low heat. Squeeze the soaked gelatine sheet to remove most of the water, then stir it into the warm mixture until it completely dissolves.

Pour one-third of the chicken consommé-gelatine mixture into a terrine mould, then add the drained Chinese wolfberries. Refrigerate it for 2 minutes.

Pour another one-third of the chicken consommé-gelatine mixture into the terrine mould on top of the wolfberry layer, then arrange some aubergine flesh neatly in the mould. Refrigerate it for another 2 minutes.

Pour the remaining chicken consommé-gelatine mixture into the mould and refrigerate it overnight to allow it to set.

A few hours before serving, heat a pot of water and poach the baby clam meat for a few seconds.

Heat the oil in a wok and add the poached baby clams. Season with the sugar, oyster sauce and cooking wine. Stir in the cornflour mixture to thicken the sauce, then leave it to cool before refrigerating until cold.

Slice the terrine and place on serving plates. Garnish with lemon or orange zest and the baby clams. Serve cold.

NOTE To remove any bitterness from the lemon or orange zest, bring a small pot of water to the boil. Stir in some honey and add 1–2 cinnamon sticks and a sprig of mint leaves. Leave the mixture to cool to room temperature. Poach the lemon or orange zest, then add it to the honey syrup. Leave the zest in the syrup and keep refrigerated overnight before using.

BEEF CARPACCIO WITH SAUTÉED BARLEY IN YUZU JELLY

SERVES 4

Beef tenderloin *300 g (11 oz)*

Barley *45 g (1¹/₂ oz)*

Cooking oil *1 Tbsp*

Carrot *20 g (²/₃ oz), peeled and diced*

Coriander (cilantro) stems *10 g (¹/₃ oz), diced*

Black truffle *20 g (²/₃ oz), diced*

Celery *10 g (¹/₃ oz), diced*

Salt *¹/₄ tsp*

Truffle oil *¹/₄ tsp*

Chicken consommé (see p133) *1 Tbsp*

Cornflour (cornstarch) *¹/₄ tsp, mixed with 1 tsp water*

Yuzu Jelly

Beef knuckle *200 g (7 oz), chopped*

Leek *30 g (1 oz), chopped*

Carrot *30 g (1 oz), peeled and chopped*

Onion *30 g (1 oz), peeled and chopped*

Rock sugar *10 g (¹/₃ oz)*

Kikkoman soy sauce *3 tsp*

Water *1 litre (32 fl oz / 4 cups)*

Gelatine *1 sheet, soaked in cold water for 10 minutes*

Yuzu juice *3 tsp*

Garnish

Shiso leaves *4*

Wasabi

Prepare this dish a day ahead.

Prepare the beef by wrapping it tightly with plastic wrap (cling film), then leaving it in the freezer overnight. Unwrap the beef and slice thinly just before serving.

Prepare the barley by bringing a small pot of water to the boil. When the water is boiling, add the barley and cook for 20 minutes or until the barley is tender.

Heat the oil in a wok and add the cooked, tender barley together with the carrot, coriander, truffle and celery. Stir-fry the mixture lightly, then add salt, truffle oil and chicken consommé. Stir-fry again to mix the seasoning well, then add the cornflour mixture to thicken the sauce. Remove the mixture from the heat, transfer to a small container and refrigerate it overnight.

Place all the ingredients for yuzu jelly, except gelatine and yuzu juice, in a pot and bring to the boil. Lower the heat and simmer for 1 hour, or until the quantity is reduced to 250 ml (8 fl oz / 1 cup). Strain and return the stock to the pot. Place the pot over low heat.

Meanwhile, squeeze the soaked gelatine sheet to remove most of the water, then place it into the pot together with the yuzu juice, stirring until the gelatine melts. Remove the pot from the heat and leave to cool slightly before refrigerating overnight to set the jelly. Cut the jelly into small cubes just before serving.

To serve, place a shiso leaf on a serving plate. Position a 2.5-cm (1-in) wide ring cutter on the shiso leaf, then spoon the chilled barley mixture into the ring. Press the filling down lightly to compact it, then remove ring.

Slice beef thinly and arrange on top of barley mixture. Top with yuzu jelly and wasabi. Serve immediately.

WOK-FRIED GLUTEN WITH GINGKO NUTS AND MUSHROOMS

SERVES 4

Cooking oil *for deep-frying*

Brown wheat gluten (*kao fu*) *200 g (7 oz), cut into 2.5-cm (1-in) cubes*

Ginger *2 thin slices*

Canned gingko nuts *30 g (1 oz)*

Wood ear fungus *20 g (²/₃ oz), soaked overnight*

Flowering chives *10 g (¹/₃ oz), cut into 2.5-cm (1-in) lengths*

Red bird's eye chillies *3*

Chicken consommé* *300 ml (10 fl oz / 1¹/₄ cups)*

Seasoning
Oyster sauce *3 tsp*

Dark soy sauce *¹/₂ tsp*

Chinese cooking wine (*hua tiao*) *1 tsp*

Rock sugar *30 g (1 oz)*

Garnish
Toasted white sesame seeds

Heat the oil in a wok and gently lower in the gluten cubes. Deep-fry the gluten cubes until crisp and golden brown, then remove with a wire strainer and plunge immediately into a large basin of hot water. Drain the gluten cubes and set aside.

Leave 1 Tbsp oil in the wok and add ginger slices. Stir-fry the ginger until lightly fragrant, then add the gingko nuts, wood ear fungus, chives and bird's eye chillies. Stir-fry the mixture lightly, then add the chicken consommé and seasoning ingredients. Lower the heat and simmer the mixture, uncovered, for 15 minutes.

Remove the simmered mixture from the heat and leave to cool to room temperature before refrigerating. This dish is served chilled and can be stored refrigerated for up to 1 week. Garnish with toasted sesame seeds just before serving.

NOTE If canned gingko nuts are unavailable, use the fresh variety. To prepare the fresh nuts, shell then soak the nuts in boiling water for 10 minutes. Drain and peel the skin off the nuts, then place in a small pot and cover with water. Bring the water to the boil, then lower the heat and simmer for 30 minutes until the nuts are tender. Use as required.

*CHICKEN CONSOMMÉ

MAKES ABOUT 2 LITRES (64 FL OZ / 8 CUPS)

Water *4 litres (128 fl oz / 16 cups)*

Chicken *1 kg (2 lb 3 oz)*

Lean pork *750 g (1 lb 10 oz)*

Chinese (Yunnan) ham *330 g (12 oz)*

Bring the water to the boil in a large stockpot. Add the chicken, pork and ham, then lower the heat and simmer over low heat for 8 hours, or until only about 2 litres (64 fl oz / 8 cups) of stock is left.

Strain the stock and discard the chicken, pork and ham. The stock can be kept refrigerated for up to 1 week or frozen for up to 3 months. Use as needed.

CRISPY CHICKEN FLOSS ROLL COATED WITH SESAME SEEDS AND TOPPED WITH TOMATO SALSA

SERVES 4

Cooking oil *for deep-frying*

Minced garlic *¹/₄ tsp*

Minced shallot *¹/₄ tsp*

Shiitake mushrooms *45 g (1¹/₂ oz), caps wiped and minced*

Minced chicken *100 g (3¹/₂ oz)*

Cornflour (cornstarch) *¹/₄ tsp, mixed with 1 tsp water*

Chicken floss *100 g (3¹/₂ oz)*

Wafer paper *4 sheets*

Egg yolk *¹/₂, beaten*

White sesame seeds *100 g (3¹/₂ oz)*

Seasoning

Yellow bean paste *¹/₂ tsp*

Oyster sauce *¹/₂ tsp*

Sugar *¹/₂ tsp*

Ground white pepper *¹/₄ tsp*

Chinese cooking wine (*hua tiao*) *1 tsp*

Chicken consommé (see p133) *4 Tbsp*

Salsa

Tomatoes *2, peeled, seeded and diced*

Mango *1, peeled and diced*

Truffle oil

Salt

Garnish

Black caviar

Chervil

Heat 1 Tbsp of oil in a wok and stir-fry the minced garlic and shallot until fragrant. Add the mushrooms and stir-fry lightly, then add the minced chicken and seasoning ingredients. Stir to mix well and bring the mixture to the boil. Stir in the cornflour mixture to thicken the sauce, then remove it from the heat. Transfer the mixture to a bowl, then toss with chicken floss and refrigerate it for about 30 minutes.

Remove the chicken mixture from the refrigerator and divide it into 4 equal portions. Spoon 1 portion of the mixture in a row on a sheet of wafer paper and roll it up like a spring roll. Repeat to make 4 rolls.

Heat the oil for deep-frying in a wok. Dip the rolls into the beaten egg yolk, then roll them in sesame seeds to coat them. Deep-fry the rolls for about 1 minute, or until golden brown and crisp. Remove and drain well.

Prepare the salsa. Toss the tomatoes and mango with truffle oil, then sprinkle the salt over.

Cut each roll into 3 rounds and top with salsa. Garnish with caviar and chervil and serve immediately.

CRISPY CRABMEAT PASTRY WITH FOIE GRAS BRAISED IN SOY SAUCE

SERVES 4

Dough
Plain (all-purpose) flour *125 g (4¹/₂ oz)*
Egg yolk *1*
Vegetable shortening *1 tsp*

Filling
Cooking oil *for deep-frying*
Chopped shallot *1 tsp*
Chopped spring onion (scallion) *1 tsp*
Crabmeat *85 g (3 oz)*
Leek *45 g (1¹/₂ oz), chopped*
Hard-boiled egg *1, shelled and finely chopped*
Salt *¹/₄ tsp*
Sugar *¹/₄ tsp*
Ground white pepper *¹/₄ tsp*
Truffle oil *1 tsp*

Braised Foie Gras
Cinnamon sticks *3*
Tsaoko fruit *2*
Star anise *5*
Liquorice root *2*
Onion *100 g (3¹/₂ oz), peeled and sliced*
Rock sugar *100 g (3¹/₂ oz)*
Water *3 litres (96 fl oz / 6 cups)*
Light soy sauce *100 ml (3¹/₃ fl oz)*
Chinese cooking wine (*hua tiao*) *300 ml (10 fl oz / 1¹/₄ cups)*
Foie gras *300 g (11 oz)*

Garnish
Quail eggs *4, cooked sunny side up*
Black caviar
Ginger dressing (see p138)

Prepare the braised foie gras. Place all the ingredients, except the water, light soy sauce, cooking wine and foie gras, in a small muslin bag and tie it up with kitchen string. Bring the water to the boil in a pot and place the muslin bag in the pot. Add the light soy sauce and Chinese cooking wine, then reduce to low heat and allow the mixture to simmer, covered, for about 30 minutes. Remove the pot from the heat and place the foie gras in the hot stock. Cover the pot and leave the stock to cool before refrigerating it overnight.

Remove the foie gras from the stock and mash it. Place the mashed foie gras on a sheet of plastic wrap (cling film) and roll it up tightly like a sausage. Place it in the freezer overnight.

When the foie gras is ready for serving, prepare the dough. Combine the flour, egg yolk and shortening into a dough, then roll it out into a thin sheet. Cut out 8 rounds using an 8-cm (3-in) round cutter.

Prepare the filling. Heat 1 Tbsp of oil and fry the chopped shallot until light golden. Drain well and combine it with the remaining ingredients for the filling. Divide the filling into 4 portions.

Spoon 1 portion of the filling onto the centre of a dough round and cover with another dough round. Press the edges together to seal the pastry. Repeat this step to make 4 servings.

Heat the oil for deep-frying and deep-fry the pastries for 2 minutes, or until they are crisp and golden brown. Drain the pastries well and set aside.

Remove the foie gras from the freezer and discard the plastic wrap. Slice it into 1-cm (¹/₂-in) thick rounds and place them on top of the pastries. Top the pastries with quail eggs and garnish with caviar and ginger dressing. Serve immediately.

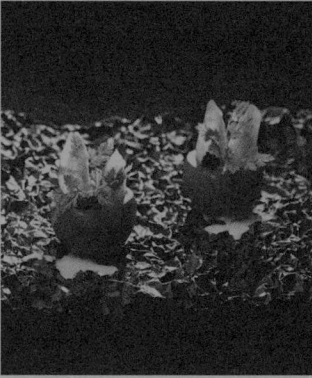

CRABMEAT AND SWEET BLACK PLUM TOSSED WITH SOUR PLUM DRESSING IN CHERRY TOMATO

Cherry tomatoes *4*

Crabmeat *30 g (1 oz)*

Sour Plum Dressing

Egg white *85 g (3 oz)*

Japanese vinegar *3 Tbsp*

Sweet prune powder *20 g (²/₃ oz)*

Lemon juice *3 tsp*

Red food colouring *2–3 drops*

Garnish

Black caviar

Chervil

Sweet black plum slices

Slice off the bottom of the tomatoes so they can sit on their own. Cut the tops off, then use a melon baller to scoop the seeds out.

Stuff the hollowed-out tomatoes with crabmeat, then garnish with caviar, chervil and sweet black plum slices. Arrange the tomatoes on a serving plate.

Prepare the dressing. Beat the egg white until smooth, then add all the remaining ingredients for the dressing and mix well. Serve the dressing with the tomatoes.

NOTE Sweet prune powder is available at the supermarkets. It is usually eaten with fresh guava slices.

SEA CUCUMBER ON JULIENNE SNOW PEAS

SERVES 4

Cooking oil *1 Tbsp*

Ginger *2 thin slices*

Spring onions (scallions) *2, trimmed and cut into short lengths*

Chicken feet *100 g (3¹/₂ oz), poached*

Chicken *150 g (5¹/₃ oz), poached*

Lean pork *150 g (5¹/₃ oz), poached*

Water *1.25 litres (40 fl oz / 5 cups)*

Oyster sauce *2 tsp*

Rock sugar *10 g (¹/₃ oz)*

Ready-prepared sea cucumber *1, small*

Snow peas *100 g (3¹/₂ oz), cut into fine julienne*

Sesame oil *¹/₄ tsp*

Salt *¹/₄ tsp*

Heat the oil in a wok and sauté the ginger and spring onions until fragrant. Add the poached chicken feet, chicken and pork and sauté lightly. Add the water, then stir in the oyster sauce and rock sugar.

Add the prepared sea cucumber and simmer, uncovered, over low heat for 30 minutes, or until the water is reduced to about 200 ml (6¹/₂ fl oz). Remove the sea cucumber and strain the stock. Return the sea cucumber to the stock, then cover and refrigerate it overnight. The stock will set into a jelly.

Just before serving, heat a pot of water and blanch the snow peas, then plunge them immediately into ice water. Drain the snow peas well, then toss with sesame oil and salt. Place the snow peas on a serving plate.

Remove the sea cucumber from the jellied stock. Cut it into 4 rings and arrange the rings on the snow peas. Mince the jelly and spoon it into the cucumber rings. Serve this dish cold.

NOTE Sea cucumbers are sold dried or ready-prepared. To prepare dried sea cucumbers, place them over an open fire and roast them until completely charred. Scrape off the burnt layer, then place them in boiling water. Remove from the heat, cover and leave the sea cucumbers to soak overnight. After soaking, remove the sea cucumbers and make a shallow cut in the underbelly. Discard the insides and wash, then soak the sea cucumbers for another 8 hours in cold water. Repeat the process of boiling the sea cucumbers and soaking them in cold water for another 2 or 3 times until the sea cucumbers are three times their original size. When preparing sea cucumbers, it is important not to allow them to come into contact with oil, or they will spoil easily. The prepared sea cucumbers can be kept frozen for up to 6 months.

CHILLED LOBSTER
WITH THREE DRESSINGS

SERVES 3

Australian lobster *1, about 800 g
(1³/₄ lb)*

Ginger Dressing
Young ginger *50 g (2 oz), peeled*
Spring onion (scallion) *50 g (2 oz)*
Vegetable oil *20 ml (²/₃ fl oz)*
Salt *¹/₄ tsp*
Sugar *¹/₄ tsp*
Sesame oil *125 ml (4 fl oz / ¹/₂ cup)*

Mango Dressing
Ripe mango *20 g (²/₃ oz), diced*
Thai sweet chilli sauce *¹/₄ tsp*
Salt *¹/₄ tsp*
Chopped chives *¹/₄ tsp*

Caviar Dressing
Sour cream *¹/₄ tsp*
Salt *¹/₄ tsp*
Truffle oil *¹/₄ tsp*
Black caviar *¹/₄ tsp*

Seaweed Powder
Dried seaweed *1 sheet, toasted
and finely ground*

To prepare the ginger dressing, place the ginger, spring onion and vegetable oil in a blender (food processor) and blend into a purée. Season it with salt, sugar and sesame oil. Leave the dressing to stand for 15–20 minutes to allow the oil to separate, then drain off the layer of excess oil. If preferred, prepare a larger portion of this dressing and keep refrigerated for up to 1 week.

Combine the ingredients for the mango dressing and set it aside.

Prepare the caviar dressing. In a small bowl, combine the sour cream, salt and truffle oil and mix well. Add the caviar and toss lightly.

Prepare the lobster. Insert a wooden chopstick into the body of the lobster and place it in a steamer over high heat for 15 minutes. This will ensure that the lobster does not curl up when cooked. Plunge the steamed lobster immediately into ice water and leave it for about 20 minutes, or until it is completely cold.

Remove the chopstick from the lobster. Remove the lobster's head and turn the lobster over, so the underside is facing up. Using a pair of kitchen scissors, make 2 long parallel cuts, one on each side of the stomach. Remove the cut section, then pull the lobster meat out. Cut the meat into 9 rounds.

Top 3 rounds with ginger dressing, another 3 with mango dressing and the remaining 3 with caviar dressing. Sprinkle all with seaweed powder and garnish as desired before serving.

NOTE The excess oil from making the ginger dressing can be used as a flavoured oil for salads.

FRESH SHARK'S FIN
IN XO SAUCE

SERVES 1

Chicken consommé (see p133)
  300 ml (10 fl oz / 1¹/₄ cups)

Salt *¹/₂ tsp*

Sugar *¹/₂ tsp*

Ready-prepared shark's fin *85 g
  (3 oz)*

Chinese cooking wine (*hua tiao*)
  85 ml (2¹/₂ fl oz / ¹/₂ cup)

Gelatine *1 sheet, soaked in cold water
  for 10 minutes*

Tiger prawn (shrimp) *1*

Sauce

Minced garlic *1 tsp, soaked in cold
  water for 15 minutes*

Cooking oil *1 Tbsp*

XO Sauce *2 tsp*

Garnish

Yellow pickled daikon

Ginger leaf

Prepare this dish a day ahead.

Bring half the chicken consommé to the boil in a small pot. Season it with
¹/₄ tsp salt and ¹/₄ tsp sugar, then add the shark's fin. Reduce the heat to
low and cook the shark's fin for 3 minutes. Drain and place the shark's fin in
a small bowl. This bowl will act as a mould for the shark's fin.

Using the same small pot, add the remaining consommé, salt and sugar
and cooking wine and bring the mixture to the boil. Drain and squeeze the
excess water from the gelatine sheet, then stir it into the consommé until it
dissolves. Pour the mixture into the bowl with the shark's fin and refrigerate
it overnight.

When ready to serve the shark's fin, prepare the sauce. Drain the minced
garlic until completely dry. Heat the oil in a wok and sauté the drained garlic
until lightly brown and fragrant. Drain and mix well with the XO sauce.

Bring a pot of water to the boil and poach the prawn. Shell the prawn and
arrange it on a serving plate. Unmould the shark's fin and arrange it with the
prawn on the serving plate. Drizzle with the sauce and garnish with pickled
daikon and ginger leaf, if desired.

NOTE Soaking the minced garlic in cold water for 15 minutes ensures that the fried
garlic will remain crisp for up to 1 week. Prepare a larger quantity and use as
needed. Store in an airtight jar.

CHAWANMUSHI WITH BLACK TRUFFLE SAUCE AND CRISPY CHEESE CRACKER

SERVES 10

Chawanmushi
Eggs *2*
Water *400 ml (13 fl oz)*
Salt *¼ tsp*
Hondashi *½ tsp*
Light soy sauce *¼ tsp*
Mirin *½ tsp*
Sake *¼ tsp*

Crispy Cheese Crackers
Parmesan cheese *300 g (11 oz), grated*

Black Truffle Sauce
Water *1 litre (32 fl oz / 4 cups)*
Chinese black truffle *55 g (2 oz), diced*
Lean pork *150 g (5⅓ oz), diced and parboiled*
Chicken *150 g (5⅓ oz), diced and parboiled*
Chicken feet *85 g (3 oz), parboiled*
Chinese (Yunnan) ham *30 g (1 oz), parboiled*
Rock sugar *1 small cube*
Truffle oil *a dash*
Oyster sauce *¼ tsp*
Cornflour (cornstarch) *¼ tsp, mixed with ½ tsp water*

Garnish
Finely diced black truffle
Chinese wolfberries *2 tsp, soaked for 10 minutes and drained*
Chervil

Prepare the crispy cheese crackers. Divide the cheese into 10 portions. Place a non-stick pan over low heat and sprinkle 1 portion of cheese into the pan. Leave it for 30 seconds until the cheese is melted and bubbling, then peel it off from the pan. Leave the melted cheese to cool on a sheet of greaseproof paper. Repeat this step to make 10 crackers. Set aside.

Prepare the black truffle sauce. Bring the water to the boil in a pot and add the truffle, pork, chicken, chicken feet and ham. Reduce to low heat and simmer for about 1 hour, or until the water is reduced to about 200 ml (6½ fl oz). Strain the stock and return it to the pot. Stir in the rock sugar, truffle oil and oyster sauce. When the rock sugar has dissolved, stir in the cornflour mixture to thicken the sauce.

Combine the ingredients for the chawanmushi, then set it aside for 10 minutes. Pour the mixture into 10 small heatproof cups and steam them for about 10 minutes, or until the chawanmushi is cooked. Scoop out some chawanmushi from the centre of each cup and pour the black truffle sauce into the hollow.

Serve the chawanmushi with the cheese crackers, garnished with truffle, wolfberries and chervil.

TEMPURA OYSTER COATED WITH LEMON CITRUS CREAM AND CRISPY SOY BEAN CRUMB

SERVES 4

Oysters *4*

Salt *¹/₄ tsp*

Tempura flour *30 g (1 oz)*

Cornflour (cornstarch) *30 g (1 oz)*

Cooking oil *for deep-frying*

Seasoning

Salted egg yolks *2, steamed and minced*

Mandarin orange segments *55 g (2 oz)*

Lemon juice *2 Tbsp*

Orange juice *2 Tbsp*

White wine *4 Tbsp*

Whipping cream *4 Tbsp*

Chicken consommé (see p133) *100 ml (3¹/₂ fl oz)*

Salt *¹/₄ tsp*

Garnish

Crispy soy bean crumb* *100 g (3¹/₂ oz)*

Garlic *1 clove, peeled and minced*

Chopped chives

Season the oysters with salt and dust with tempura flour and cornflour. Heat the oil in a wok and deep-fry the oysters until golden brown and crisp. This takes 20–30 seconds. Drain the oysters well and set aside.

Leave 1 Tbsp of oil in the wok, and fry the minced garlic for garnish until light golden brown. Remove it from the oil and drain well.

In a clean wok, heat 1 Tbsp of oil and fry the steamed salted egg yolks until they are bubbly. Add the remaining seasoning ingredients until heated through, then toss in the fried oysters. Mix well.

To serve, coat the oysters with the crispy soy bean crumb if desired, then garnish with garlic and chives.

NOTE If soy bean crumb is not available, use minced garlic. To prepare the minced garlic, heat 2 Tbsp of oil and fry 100 g (3¹/₂ oz) of minced garlic until light golden brown and crisp. Drain well on paper towels. When the minced garlic is cool and dry, store in an airtight container at room temperature. It can keep for up to 1 week.

*CRISPY SOY BEAN CRUMB

MAKES ABOUT 100 G (3¹/₂ OZ)

Soy bean crumb *100 g (3¹/₂ oz)*

Cooking oil *2 Tbsp*

Steam the soy bean crumb for about 15 minutes, then chop it up until fine. Heat the oil in a wok and fry the steamed soy bean crumb until crisp. Remove from the oil and drain well. When the soy bean crumb is cool and dry, store it in an airtight container. It can keep for up to 1 week.

SERVES 4

Chicken consommé (see p133)
  100 ml (3¹/₃ fl oz)

Salt *¹/₂ tsp*

White asparagus *12 spears, cut into*
  8-cm (3-in) lengths

Sri Lankan crab *1, about 400 g*
  (14¹/₃ oz), cleaned

Ginger dressing (see p138)

Garnish
Shiso leaves

Seaweed powder (see p138)

WHITE ASPARAGUS WITH CRABMEAT IN GINGER DRESSING

Prepare this dish a day ahead.

Bring the chicken consommé to the boil in a small shallow pan. Sprinkle in the salt, then place the asparagus in to cook for 3 minutes, or until they are tender. Drain the asparagus and store refrigerated overnight.

Place the crab in a steamer and steam until the crab is cooked. Crack the shell, remove the flesh and refrigerate the flesh until it is cold.

To serve, place 3 asparagus spears on each serving plate and top with some crabmeat. Spoon some ginger dressing over and garnish with shiso leaves and seaweed powder.

STEAMED CRAB CLAW WITH YUNNAN HAM AND GINGER

Cooking oil *1 Tbsp*

Chinese (Yunnan) ham *100 g (3¹/₂ oz), minced*

Ginger *55 (2 oz), peeled and minced*

Chicken consommé (see p133) *200 ml (6¹/₂ fl oz)*

Salt *¼ tsp*

Sugar *¼ tsp*

Chinese cooking wine (*hua tiao*) *1 tsp*

Cornflour (cornstarch) *¹/₂ tsp, mixed with 1 tsp water*

Crab claws *4, large, cracked and shelled*

Heat the oil in a wok and add ham, ginger and chicken consommé. When the consommé comes to the boil, season it with salt, sugar and Chinese cooking wine. Stir in the cornflour mixture to thicken the stock.

Place the crab claws in 4 small heatproof bowls and ladle the thickened stock over. Place the bowls in a steamer and steam for 6 minutes. Serve this dish hot.

Soups

DOUBLE-BOILED PRAWN DUMPLING IN HOT AND SOUR CONSOMMÉ

SERVES 4

Dumpling

Glutinous rice flour *200 g (7 oz)*

Cold water *30 g (1 oz)*

Peeled prawns (shrimps) *100 g (3½ oz)*

Water chestnuts *3, peeled and minced*

Coriander (cilantro) stem *5 g (⅙ oz), minced*

Egg white *¼*

Sugar *½ tsp*

Salt *⅓ tsp*

Ground white pepper *⅛ tsp*

Sesame oil *½ tsp*

Cornflour (cornstarch) *½ tsp*

Morel Consommé

Morels *100 g (3½ oz)*

Chicken breast *100 g (3½ oz), minced*

Egg white *1, lightly beaten*

Egg shell *1, crushed*

Celery *30 g (1 oz), minced*

Carrot *30 g (1 oz)*

Bird's eye chilli *1*

Bay leaf *1*

White peppercorns *30 g (1 oz)*

Chicken consommé (see p133) *1 litre (32 fl oz / 4 cups)*

Salt *to taste*

Tabasco sauce *20 ml (⅔ fl oz)*

White vinegar *30 ml (1 fl oz)*

Garnish

Seaweed powder (see p138)

Prepare the dumpling dough. Combine the glutinous rice flour and cold water to form a dough. Roll the dough into a cylinder about 2.5 cm (1 in) in diameter and cut into 4 pieces, each about 2.5 cm (1 in) long. Discard any excess dough. Roll each dough piece into a ball and flatten into a thin round using a rolling pin. Cover the dough rounds to prevent them from drying out while preparing the filling.

Mince the peeled prawns using a cleaver until the mixture is pasty. Add the remaining ingredients for the filling and mix well. Divide the mixture into 4 portions.

Spoon 1 portion onto the centre of a dough round. Bring the edges of the dough up to enclose the filling, then roll into a ball. Repeat this step to make 4 dumplings in total.

Bring a small pot of water to the boil and cook the dumplings for 2 minutes, or until the dumplings float to the surface. Drain and set the dumplings aside.

Combine all the ingredients for the morel consommé except the salt, Tabasco sauce and white vinegar in a pot. Bring to the boil over low heat, then simmer, uncovered, for about 1 hour, or until the consommé is reduced to about 600 ml (20 fl oz / 2½ cups).

Strain the morel consommé, being careful not to agitate the solids or the consommé will turn cloudy. Season the consommé with the salt, Tabasco sauce and white vinegar. The morel consommé should be both hot and sour. Add more seasoning as necessary.

Garnish the dumplings with seaweed powder. Serve the morel consommé with the dumplings on the side.

STEAMED CRAB CLAW WITH BAMBOO PITHS AND CORDYCEPS IN SUPERIOR CHICKEN CONSOMMÉ

SERVES 4

Bamboo piths *8, soaked overnight and drained*

Cordyceps *8, soaked for 10 minutes and drained*

Crab claws *4, large, cracked and shelled*

Superior Chicken Consommé

Water *4 litres (128 fl oz / 16 cups)*

Chicken *1 whole, about 2 kg (4 lb 6 oz), cleaned, cut into 8 pieces and parboiled*

Salt *¹/₂ tsp*

Sugar *¹/₂ tsp*

Ground white pepper *¹/₄ tsp*

Chinese cooking wine (*hua tiao*) *1 tsp*

Garnish

Seaweed powder (see p138)

Prepare the superior chicken consommé. Bring the water to the boil in a large pot and add the parboiled chicken pieces. Cook over high heat, uncovered, for 15 minutes until the water is cloudy. Lower the heat and simmer, uncovered, for 3 hours until the liquid is reduced to 1 litre (32 fl oz / 4 cups). Season the consommé with salt, sugar, pepper and Chinese wine.

Place the bamboo piths and cordyceps in 4 heatproof bowls. Pour enough consommé over to cover the ingredients, then place the bowls in a steamer and steam for 30 minutes.

Steam the crab claws for 6 minutes, then place them into the freshly steamed bowls of bamboo piths and cordyceps.

Garnish with seaweed powder and serve hot.

BRAISED TOMATO CONFIT WITH BABY ABALONE IN TOMATO BROTH

SERVES 4

Canned baby abalone *1 can (contains 12 abalones, each about 25 g (1 oz))*

Tomatoes *4*

Tomato Broth

Tomatoes *3, diced*

Potatoes *2, peeled and diced*

Celery *30 g (1 oz), diced*

Onion *30 g (1 oz), peeled and diced*

Tomato paste *3 Tbsp*

White peppercorns *5*

Bay leaf *1*

Water *2 litres (64 fl oz / 8 cups)*

Salt *¹/₂ tsp*

Chinese cooking wine (*hua tiao*) *2 tsp*

Abalone juice (from canned abalone)

Garnish

Black truffle *4 thin slices*

Place the unopened can of baby abalones in a steamer and steam for 2 hours. This recipe only requires 4 baby abalones, but you may wish to increase the number of abalones for each serving, or use them in other soup dishes.

Cut a shallow 'X' on the bottom of the tomatoes and steam them for about 5 minutes. This makes it easier to peel them. Slowly peel the skins off the tomatoes, then cut the tops off and scoop out the seeds.

Place the tomatoes in small heatproof serving bowls, then place a baby abalone in each tomato. Add more abalones as desired.

Combine all the ingredients for the tomato broth in a pot and bring to the boil. Lower the heat and simmer the broth for about 1 hour, uncovered, until the broth is thick and reduced to about 300 ml (10 fl oz / 1¹/₄ cups). When the broth is ready, strain it through a fine sieve, then pour a ladleful over the tomato in each bowl.

Place the bowls in a steamer and steam for 5 minutes. Serve this dish garnished with thinly sliced black truffle.

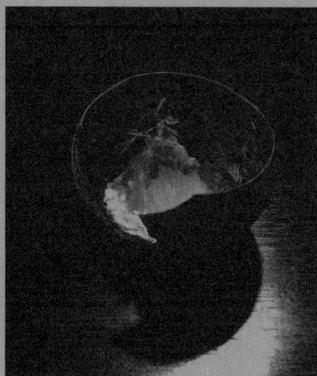

SHARK'S FIN WITH ALASKAN CRABMEAT IN EGG WHITE SAUCE

SERVES 4

Chicken consommé (see p133) *1 litre (32 fl oz / 4 cups)*

Salt *1 tsp*

Sugar *1 tsp*

Ready-prepared shark's fin *320 g (11½ oz)*

Alaskan crab claws *4*

Cooking oil *½ Tbsp*

Chinese cooking wine (*hua tiao*) *2 tsp*

Cornflour (cornstarch) *3 tsp, mixed with 1 Tbsp water*

Egg whites *2, lightly beaten*

Garnish

Chervil

Bring half the chicken consommé to the boil. Stir in ½ tsp salt and ½ tsp sugar, then add the shark's fin and cook over low heat for 3 minutes. Drain the shark's fin and divide it into 4 portions. Place each portion in a small heatproof bowl.

Place a crab claw on top of each portion of shark's fin and steam for about 3 minutes.

Heat the oil in a wok. Add the remaining chicken consommé and bring to a simmer until just heated through. Season the consommé with the remaining salt and sugar and Chinese cooking wine.

Stir in the cornflour mixture to thicken the sauce, then add the egg whites. The egg whites will cook very quickly. Pour this mixture over the steamed shark's fin, garnish with chervil and serve immediately.

NOTE Cooked Alaskan crab is available from the frozen section of supermarkets.

JULIENNE CHICKEN, SNOW PEAS, YUNNAN HAM AND DRIED SCALLOPS IN SUPERIOR BROTH

SERVES 4

Chicken breast *200 g (7 oz)*

Chinese (Yunnan) ham *100 g (3¹/₂ oz), cut into fine julienne*

Snow peas *85 g (3 oz)*

Cooking oil *1 Tbsp*

Young spinach *¹/₂ small bunch, rinsed and blanched*

Scallops

Dried scallops *85 g (3 oz), soaked overnight and drained*

Chicken consommé (see p133) *as needed*

Salt *¹/₄ tsp*

Cooking oil *1 tsp*

Ginger *1 thin slice*

Spring onion (scallion) *1, trimmed and cut into short lengths*

Superior Consommé

Water *5 litres (8 pints / 20 cups)*

Lean pork *300 g (11 oz), parboiled*

Chicken *300 g (11 oz), parboiled*

Chicken feet *100 g (3¹/₂ oz), parboiled*

Pork bones *300 g (11 oz), parboiled*

Carrots *100 g (3¹/₂ oz), cut into chunks*

Seasoning

Salt *¹/₄ tsp*

Sugar *¹/₄ tsp*

Chinese cooking wine (*hua tiao*) *¹/₄ tsp*

Cornflour (cornstarch) *1 tsp, mixed with 3 tsp water*

Prepare the superior consommé. Bring the water to the boil in a large pot. Add all the remaining ingredients for the consommé and cook over high heat for about 15 minutes, or until the consommé is cloudy. Lower the heat and simmer the consommé, uncovered, for 2 hours, or until the liquid is reduced to about 1.5 litres (48 fl oz / 6 cups). Strain the consommé and discard the ingredients.

While waiting for the superior consommé to reduce, steam the chicken breast meat and Chinese ham. Shred the chicken meat finely and set aside.

Cut the snow peas into fine strips, then blanch them in lightly salted water.

Prepare the dried scallops. Drain the soaked scallops and place them in a small heatproof bowl. Add enough chicken consommé to cover the scallops, then add the salt, cooking oil, ginger and spring onion. Place the bowl into a steamer and steam for about 45 minutes, or until the scallops are tender. Shred the scallops finely and set aside.

Heat the oil in a wok and add the superior consommé and seasoning ingredients. Simmer until heated through.

To serve, place an 8-cm (3-in) wide ring cutter in a heatproof bowl. Spoon a layer of shredded chicken into the ring, followed by snow peas, ham and scallops. Press the ingredients down to compact them, then place the bowl together with the ring cutter in a steamer and steam for 2 minutes. Remove the ring cutter and repeat to make 4 servings in total.

Ladle some superior consommé around the mound of ingredients and garnish with blanched spinach leaves. Serve this dish hot.

CHILLED MOREL CONSOMMÉ

SERVES 4

Barley *1 Tbsp*

Lotus seeds *20*

Chinese wolfberries *1 Tbsp, soaked
    for 10 minutes and drained*

Black truffle slices

Morel Consommé

Dried morels *100 g (3¹/₂ oz), soaked
    overnight and rinsed*

Minced chicken *100 g (3¹/₂ oz)*

Egg white *1*

Egg shell *1, crushed*

Celery *30 g (1 oz)*

Carrot *30 g (1 oz), peeled and minced*

Bay leaf *1*

Ground white pepper *¹/₄ tsp*

Chicken consommé (see p133)
    1 litre (32 fl oz / 4 cups)

Salt *¹/₄ tsp*

Combine all the ingredients for the morel consommé, except the salt, in a pot and simmer, covered, for 3 hours. Strain the consommé through a muslin cloth, being careful not to agitate the solids or the consommé will become cloudy. Season the consommé to taste with salt and leave to cool slightly before refrigerating it for 3–4 hours.

Sift through the strained solids from the consommé and pick out the morels. Discard all the other ingredients. Refrigerate the morels.

Prepare the barley. Bring a pot of water to the boil. Add the barley and cook for 20 minutes, or until the barley is cooked and tender. Drain and refrigerate the barley.

Prepare the lotus seeds. Wash the lotus seeds and place them in a pot. Add enough hot water to cover the lotus seeds, then cover and steam them for 30 minutes, or until the seeds are tender. Using a toothpick, push the bitter shoots in the centre of the lotus seeds out to remove them. Refrigerate the seeds.

When all the ingredients are sufficiently chilled, spoon some consommé into a tall serving glass. Add some wolfberries, barley, truffle slices and lotus seeds, separating each ingredient with a layer of consommé. Repeat to make 4 servings. Garnish as desired and serve chilled.

Fish and Seafood

SERVES 4

Australian lobster *1, about 800 g (1³/₄ lb)*

Cooking oil *2 Tbsp*

Garlic *160 g (5²/₃ oz), peeled and minced*

Salt *¹/₂ tsp*

Sugar *¹/₂ tsp*

Sesame oil *¹/₄ tsp*

Cornflour (cornstarch) *¹/₄ tsp*

Chopped chives

<u>Sauce</u>

Cooking oil *2 Tbsp*

Ginger *1 clove, peeled and sliced*

Spring onion (scallion) *1, cut into short lengths*

Coriander leaves (cilantro) *2 sprigs*

Chicken consommé *(see p133) 100 ml (3¹/₃ fl oz)*

Light soy sauce *4 tsp*

Rock sugar *10 g (¹/₃ oz)*

Dark soy sauce *¹/₄ tsp*

STEAMED AUSTRALIAN LOBSTER WITH FRESH AND FRIED GARLIC IN FLAVOURED SAUCE

Prepare the sauce. Heat the oil in a wok and sauté the ginger and spring onion until fragrant. Add the remaining ingredients for the sauce and bring to the boil. Remove the sauce from the heat and set aside.

Prepare the lobster. Lay the lobster on its stomach. Insert the tip of a chef's knife into the base of its head, then split the head in half. Turn the lobster over, so it lies on its back. Cut through the shell to split the body in half, lengthwise, then cut each half into 2 pieces. Place the lobster on a steaming plate.

Heat the oil in a wok and fry half the garlic until crisp and golden brown. Set the garlic aside.

Combine the remaining minced garlic with salt, sugar, sesame oil and cornflour. Sprinkle the mixture over the prepared lobster and steam for about 7 minutes, or until the lobster shell turns red and the lobster is cooked.

Sprinkle the deep-fried garlic over the lobster and drizzle the sauce over. Serve the lobster hot, garnished with chopped chives.

WOK-FRIED BAMBOO CLAMS WITH **BLACK BEANS** AND ROASTED GARLIC

SERVES 4

Cooking oil *1 Tbsp*

Bamboo clams *4, shelled and cut into cubes*

Garlic *100 g (3¹/₂ oz), peeled*

Minced red chilli *¹/₂ tsp*

Minced spring onion (scallion) *¹/₂ tsp*

Minced shallot *¹/₂ tsp*

Minced ginger *¹/₂ tsp*

Salted black beans *2 tsp*

Crispy soy bean crumb (see p141) or fried minced garlic *85 g (3 oz)*

Chicken consommé (see p133) *120 ml (4 fl oz)*

Oyster sauce *2 tsp*

Sugar *1 tsp*

Cooking wine (*hua tiao*) *1 tsp*

Cornflour (cornstarch) *¹/₄ tsp, mixed with ¹/₂ tsp water*

Garnish

Red shiso cress

Seaweed powder (see p138)

Heat the oil in a wok and lightly sear the clams. Remove from the heat and set aside.

Leaving about ½ tsp oil in the wok, stir-fry the garlic, minced chilli, spring onion, shallot, ginger, salted black beans and crispy soy bean crumb until the mixture is fragrant.

Add the seared bamboo clams, chicken consommé, oyster sauce, sugar, cooking wine and bring to the boil.

When the sauce is boiling, stir in the cornflour mixture to thicken the sauce.

Serve this dish hot, garnished with shiso cress and seaweed powder.

TEMPURA LYCHEE STUFFED WITH CURRIED CRABMEAT

SERVES 4

Cooking oil *for deep-frying*

Crabmeat *40 g (1¹/₂ oz)*

Fresh lychees *4, peeled and seeded*

Cornflour (cornstarch) *20 g (²/₃ oz)*

Onion *20 g (²/₃ oz), peeled and cut into fine julienne*

Carrot *20 g (²/₃ oz), peeled and cut into fine julienne*

Enokitake mushrooms *20 g (²/₃ oz)*

Thai asparagus *12 spears, cut into fine julienne*

Seasoning

Chicken consommé (see p133) *4 Tbsp*

Seafood curry powder *¹/₄ tsp*

Salt *¹/₂ tsp*

Sugar *¹/₄ tsp*

Cornflour (cornstarch) *¹/₄ tsp, mixed with 1 tsp water*

Batter

Plain (all-purpose) flour *60 g (2 oz)*

Wheat flour (high gluten) *15 g (¹/₂ oz)*

Baking powder *10 g (¹/₃ oz)*

Custard powder *3 g (¹/₁₀ oz)*

Water *30 ml (1 fl oz)*

Cooking oil *20 ml (²/₃ fl oz)*

Garnish

Black ebiko

Heat 1 Tbsp oil in a wok. Add the crabmeat and seasoning ingredients, except the cornflour and mix well. When the mixture is heated through, stir in the cornflour mixture to thicken the sauce. Remove from the heat and set aside to cool. When the mixture is cool, refrigerate for about 1 hour, or until it is cold.

When the crabmeat is sufficiently chilled, prepare the lychees. Dust the inside of the lychees lightly with cornflour and stuff them with the chilled crabmeat.

Combine the ingredients for the batter. Add the onion, carrot, enokitake mushrooms and asparagus, and mix well with the batter. Divide the mixture into 4 portions.

Heat the oil for deep-frying.

Wrap each lychee with a portion of the batter-covered ingredients and deep-fry them immediately until they are crisp and golden brown. Drain well and serve the lychees hot, garnished with black ebiko.

Scallops *4*
Cornflour (cornstarch) *for dusting*

Mango Sauce
Ripe mango *1, peeled, seeded, diced*
Mango juice *100 ml (3¹/₃ fl oz)*
Pumpkin *30 g (1 oz)*
Whipping cream *20 ml (²/₃ fl oz)*
White wine *20 ml (²/₃ fl oz)*
Salt *¹/₄ tsp*
Sake *1 tsp*
Rosemary leaf *1*
Bay leaf *1, small*

Poached Pear
Pear *1*
Water *300 ml (10 fl oz / 1¹/₄ cups)*
Cinnamon stick *1*
Bay leaf *1*
Honey *50 ml (2 fl oz)*
White wine *2 Tbsp*

Garnish
Seaweed powder (see p138)
Minced Chinese (Yunnan) ham

SEARED SCALLOP STUFFED WITH PEAR IN WARM MANGO SAUCE

Slice the scallops horizontally in half and set them aside.

Prepare the poached pear. Pare the pear. Bring the water, cinnamon stick, bay leaf, honey and wine to the boil in a pot. Add the pear and simmer over low heat for about 30 minutes. Remove the pear and leave it aside to cool. Cut the pear into 4 slices, then cut out 4 rounds using a ring cutter of a size similar to the scallops.

Sprinkle cornflour on the cut side of the scallops and place a slice of pear between the two halves of each scallop. Transfer to a steamer and steam them for about 1 minute, then sear them immediately in a hot pan with a little oil.

Prepare the mango sauce. Blend (process) the mango flesh and juice into a smooth paste using a blender, then pour the paste into a pot together with the remaining sauce ingredients. Simmer the sauce over low heat for about 10 minutes, or until the sauce is thick. Strain the sauce to give it an even smoother texture.

Serve the scallops with the mango sauce, garnished with a sprinkling of seaweed powder and minced Chinese ham.

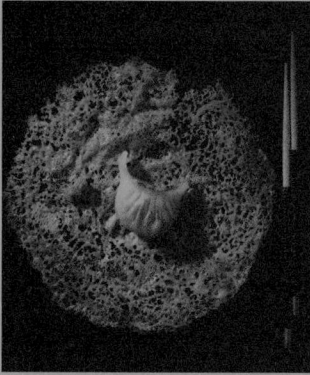

CRISPY PAN-SEARED CRABMEAT DUMPLING

Dough

Plain (all-purpose) flour *120 g (4¹/₂ oz)*

Cornflour (cornstarch) *20 g (²/₃ oz)*

Egg yolk *1*

Vegetable shortening *1 tsp*

Filling

Crabmeat *80 g (3 oz)*

Leek *40 g (1¹/₂ oz), chopped*

Chopped shallots *1 tsp*

Chopped spring onion (scallion) *1 tsp*

Salt *¹/₄ tsp*

Sugar *¹/₄ tsp*

Ground white pepper *¹/₄ tsp*

Sesame oil *¹/₄ tsp*

Crispy Cracker

Potato flour *20 g (²/₃ oz)*

Plain (all-purpose) flour *50 g (2 oz)*

Egg yolk *¹/₂*

Water *500 ml (16 fl oz / 2 cups)*

Salt *¹/₄ tsp*

Condiment (Optional)

Ginger dressing (see p138)

Combine the ingredients for the dough and knead it into a smooth, pliable dough. Roll the dough into a cylinder about 2.5 cm (1 in) in diameter, then cut it into 2.5-cm (1-in) lengths. Roll the dough pieces into balls and discard the excess dough. Using a rolling pin, roll the dough balls out into thin rounds.

Combine the ingredients for the filling and divide it into 4 portions. Spoon a portion onto each dough skin. Bring the edges of the dough skin up and pleat the edges to seal the dumpling and enclose the filling. Steam the dumplings for 2 minutes.

Meanwhile, combine the ingredients for the crispy cracker and mix well.

Heat a frying pan with 3 Tbsp oil and add a large ladle of batter into the pan. Cook the cracker for 2 minutes, or until it is lightly browned. Place a steamed dumpling on the centre of the cracker and leave it for another minute. Remove the dumpling and cracker, being careful not to break the cracker. Place it on paper towels to drain. Repeat this step with the remaining dumplings.

Serve the dumplings with ginger dressing, if desired.

SCRAMBLED EGG WITH SHARK'S FIN AND CRABMEAT

SERVES 4

Hairy or flower crabs *4, each about 200 g (7 oz), cleaned*

Japanese seaweed (*nori*) *4 sheets*

Egg white *1, beaten*

Paprika *for dusting*

Cooking oil *for deep-frying*

Ready-prepared shark's fin *60 g (2 oz)*

Scrambled Egg

Eggs *4*

Salt *1¹/₂ tsp*

Sugar *1 tsp*

Ground white pepper *¹/₈ tsp*

Cooking oil *2 tsp*

Garnish

Black caviar

Red shiso cress

Steam the cleaned crabs for 7 minutes. Leave them to cool, then shell them and remove the crabmeat. Discard the shells and set the meat aside.

Brush the seaweed sheets lightly with egg white, then sprinkle some paprika over. Heat the oil for deep-frying and deep-fry the seaweed sheets until they are crisp. Remove them carefully and drain well.

Combine the ingredients for the scrambled egg, then add the shark's fin and crabmeat. Mix well.

Heat 1 Tbsp of oil in a non-stick pan. Pour the scrambled egg mixture in and swirl the mixture so that it coats the base of the pan. Remove the egg from the heat once it is lightly set.

Divide the scrambled egg into 4 portions and spoon each portion into a 3-cm (1¹/₂-in) wide ring cutter. Press the scrambled egg down lightly to compact it, then remove the ring. Carefully transfer the scrambled egg onto the sheets of seaweed and serve immediately, garnished with caviar and shiso cress.

WOK-FRIED CRABMEAT AND ROE WITH EGG WHITE

SERVES 4

Hairy or flower crabs with roe *4, each about 200 g (7 oz), cleaned*

Puff pastry *4 sheets, each 6 x 6-cm (2.5 x 2.5-in)*

Cooking oil *1 Tbsp*

Egg White
Egg whites *2*
Fresh milk *8 tsp*
Salt *¹/₃ tsp*
Cornflour (cornstarch) *¹/₄ tsp*

Garnish
Seaweed powder (see p138)
Black vinegar

Steam the cleaned crabs for 7 minutes. Leave them to cool, then shell them and remove the crabmeat and roe. Discard the shells and set the meat and roe aside.

Place the puff pastry squares in a preheated oven at 220°C (440°F) for 10–15 minutes, or until they are puffed and golden brown.

Combine the ingredients for the egg white and add the crabmeat and roe.

Heat the oil in a non-stick pan. Pour in the egg white and crabmeat mixture and swirl the mixture so it coats the base of the pan. Cook until the egg white mixture is lightly set, then quickly remove it from the pan. Divide the mixture into 4 portions and place each portion immediately onto the puff pastry squares.

Garnish with seaweed powder and drizzle with black vinegar. Serve immediately.

CRISPY MARBLE GOBY WITH MANGO AND SWEET CHILLI SAUCE

Cooking oil *for deep-frying*

Marble goby fillets *4, each about 100 g (3¹/₂ oz), boneless, with skin*

Tapioca flour *55 g (2 oz)*

Ripe mango *1, peeled and diced*

Sweet Chilli Sauce

Red chillies *20 g (²/₃ oz), seeded and minced*

Garlic *20 g (²/₃ oz), peeled and minced*

Torch ginger bud *20 g (²/₃ oz), minced*

Coriander (cilantro) stems *20 g (²/₃ oz), minced*

Yuzu juice *4 tsp*

Water *4 Tbsp*

Honey *4 Tbsp*

Thai fish sauce *4 tsp*

Sweet Thai chilli sauce *1 Tbsp*

Combine the ingredients for the sweet chilli sauce and set it aside.

Heat the oil for deep-frying.

Make criss-cross cuts on the skinless side of the fish fillets, then dust them with tapioca flour. Deep-fry the fish fillets for about 1 minute, or until the fillets are crisp and golden brown. Remove and drain well.

Place a spoonful of diced mango on each of 4 serving plates. Arrange the fried fish fillets on top and drizzle with the sweet chilli sauce. Serve immediately.

Yabbies *4*

Dumpling Dough

Wheat starch (dim sum flour) *100 g (3¹/₂ oz)*

Hot water *50 ml (1²/₃ fl oz)*

Filling

Shelled prawns (shrimps) *150 g (5¹/₃ oz)*

Peeled water chestnuts *20 g (²/₃ oz), diced*

Dried Chinese mushrooms *10 g (¹/₃ oz), soaked to soften, then drained and diced*

Coriander (cilantro) stem *10 g (¹/₃ oz), minced*

Egg white *¹/₄, beaten*

Sugar *¹/₄ tsp*

Salt *¹/₄ tsp*

Sesame oil *¹/₄ tsp*

Ground white pepper *¹/₄ tsp*

Cornflour (cornstarch) *¹/₄ tsp*

Garnish

Black caviar

Ebiko

Chervil

STEAMED YABBY DUMPLING

Prepare the filling. Mince the shelled prawns using the spine of a cleaver until the mixture is pasty. Add all the remaining ingredients and mix well. Divide the filling into 4 portions and set aside.

Steam the yabbies for about 3 minutes, or until the colour changes and the yabbies are cooked. Shell the yabbies and set them aside.

Prepare the dumpling dough. Combine the wheat starch and water into a dough. Roll the dough into a cylinder about 1 cm (¹/₂ in) in diameter, then cut into 1-cm (¹/₂-in) lengths. Use only 4 portions. Discard the excess dough.

Using a rolling pin, flatten each portion of dough into a thin round. Spoon a portion of filling onto each dough round, then top with a shelled yabby. Bring the edges of the dough up around the filling, leaving the top open to expose the filling.

Place the dumplings in a steamer and steam for about 4 minutes, or until the dough is cooked. Garnish with caviar, ebiko and chervil. Serve the dumplings immediately.

Traditional Siew Mai

Prawns (shrimps) *8, small*

Minced pork belly *100 g (3¹/₂ oz)*

Water chestnuts *4*

Minced coriander (cilantro) stem
   ¹/₄ tsp

Salt *¹/₄ tsp*

Sugar *¹/₄ tsp*

Sesame oil *¹/₄ tsp*

Beaten egg white *¹/₄ tsp*

Ground white pepper *¹/₄ tsp*

Cornflour (cornstarch) *¹/₄ tsp, mixed
   with 1 tsp water*

Siew mai skins *4*

XO Sauce

Modern Siew Mai

Prawns (shrimps) *4, large*

Crabmeat *45 g (1¹/₂ oz)*

Water chestnuts *4, peeled and minced*

Minced coriander (cilantro) stem
   ¹/₂ tsp

Salt *¹/₂ tsp*

Sugar *¹/₂ tsp*

Sesame oil *¹/₂ tsp*

Beaten egg white *¹/₂ tsp*

Ground white pepper *¹/₂ tsp*

Scallops *4*

Cornflour (cornstarch) *¹/₂ tsp*

Pink peppercorns

Seasoning

Chicken consommé (see p133)
   4 Tbsp

Tomato paste *3 tsp*

Tomato *¹/₂, small, peeled and diced*

Salt *¹/₄ tsp*

Cornflour (cornstarch) *¹/₄ tsp, mixed
   with 1 tsp water*

TRADITIONAL AND MODERN SIEW MAI

Prepare the traditional *siew mai*. Peel the prawns, them mince them using the spine of a cleaver until the mixture is pasty. Add all the remaining ingredients except the *siew mai* skins and mix well. Divide the filling into 4 portions. Spoon a portion of the filling onto the centre of each *siew mai* skin, then bring the edges of the skin up to enclose the filling, leaving the top open and the filling exposed. Place the *siew mai* in a steamer and steam them for about 4 minutes or until the *siew mai* is cooked. Top the traditional *siew mai* with XO sauce before serving.

Combine all the ingredients for the seasoning except the cornflour mixture in a small pot and bring it to the boil. When the mixture is boiling, stir in the cornflour mixture to thicken the sauce.

Prepare the modern *siew mai*. Peel the prawns, them mince them using the spine of a cleaver until the mixture is pasty. Mix well with the remaining ingredients except the scallops and cornflour. Divide the mixture into 4 portions. Using the flat side of a cleaver, smash the scallops one at a time into flat rounds. Spoon one portion of filling onto each scallop round and bring the edge of the scallop up around the filling, leaving the top open and the filling exposed. Steam the *siew mai* for about 5 minutes, then place them top down on a hot, oiled pan and sear lightly.

Spoon some seasoning onto a serving plate and place the modern *siew mai* on top, garnished with pink peppercorns. Serve hot with the traditional *siew mai*.

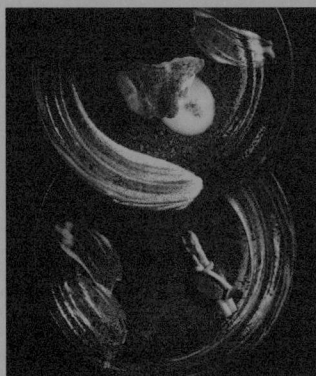

MARBLE GOBY IN MILKY CHICKEN CONSOMMÉ WITH ASPARAGUS, BLACK TRUFFLE AND ENOKI MUSHROOM

SERVES 4

Cooking oil *2 Tbsp*

Marble goby *4 fillets, each about 100 g (3¹/₂ oz), boneless, with skin*

Cornflour (cornstarch) *2 Tbsp*

Thai asparagus *12 spears*

Enokitake mushrooms *4, trimmed*

Milky Consommé

Butter *1 Tbsp*

Chicken consommé (see p133) *180 ml (6 fl oz / ³/₄ cup)*

Fresh milk *8 tsp*

Minced black truffle *2 tsp*

Truffle oil *1 tsp*

Salt *¹/₂ tsp*

Sugar *¹/₂ tsp*

Chinese cooking wine (*hua tiao*) *1 tsp*

Cornflour (cornstarch) *1 tsp, mixed with 2 tsp water*

Garnish

Black truffle *4 slices*

Seaweed powder (see p138)

Heat the oil in a wok. Dust the fish skins with cornflour and sear them, skin side down until the skin is crisp and golden brown. Place the fish fillets on a steaming plate and steam them for 3 minutes. Set aside.

Bring a pot of lightly salted water to the boil. Place the asparagus and mushrooms in for a few seconds, then remove and drain well. Tie 3 asparagus spears together using a mushroom. Steam the asparagus bundles for 1 minute.

Prepare the milky consommé. Heat the butter in a clean wok and add the chicken consommé, milk, truffle and truffle oil. Season with salt, sugar and cooking wine. When the mixture is lightly heated, stir in the cornflour mixture to thicken the consommé.

Serve the fish and asparagus with sauce on the side. Garnish with black truffle slices and seaweed powder.

BAKED COD FILLET WITH SCRAMBLED EGG WHITE

SERVES 4

Cod fillets *4, each about 100 g (3¹/₂ oz)*

Marinade
Light soy sauce *4 Tbsp*
Water *3 Tbsp*
Dark soy sauce *4 tsp*
Sugar *2 tsp*
Maggi seasoning *2 tsp*

Scrambled Egg White
Cooking oil *1 tsp*
Salt *¹/₄ tsp*
Ground white pepper *¹/₄ tsp*
Egg whites *2*
Fresh milk *6 Tbsp*

Combine the ingredients for the marinade. Place the cod fillets in the marinade and leave them for 15 minutes before transferring them to a baking tray. Bake the fillets in a preheated oven at 150°C (300°F) for 10 minutes, then reduce the heat to 100°C (210°F) and bake for a further 10 minutes.

Combine the ingredients for the scrambled egg white. Heat a non-stick pan and pour in the egg white mixture. Cook as you would a scrambled egg. Remove from the heat and divide the scrambled egg white into 4 portions. Top with the cod fillets and garnish as desired. Serve immediately.

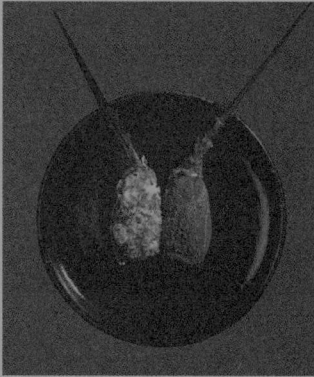

WOK-FRIED LOBSTER WITH SALTED EGG YOLK

SERVES 4

Lobster *1, about 800 g (1³/₄ lb)*

Cornflour (cornstarch) *55 g (2 oz)*

Salted egg yolks *8*

Chicken oil *1 tsp*

Curry leaves *20 g (²/₃ oz)*

Shallots *20 g (²/₃ oz), peeled and minced*

Ginger *20 g (²/₃ oz), peeled and minced*

Torch ginger bud *20 g (²/₃ oz), minced*

Chicken consommé (see p133) *100 ml (3²/₃ fl oz)*

Seafood curry powder *1 tsp*

Sugar *1 tsp*

Salt *¹/₄ tsp*

Sweetened condensed milk *1 tsp*

Garnish
Minced and roasted shallots

Chopped chives

Prepare the lobster. Lay the lobster on its stomach. Insert the tip of a chef's knife into the base of its head, then split the head in half. Turn the lobster over, so it lies on its back. Cut through the shell to split the body section in half, lengthwise, then cut each half into 2 pieces.

Heat the oil for deep-frying.

Coat the lobster with cornflour and deep-fry until it is golden brown. Remove the lobster and drain well.

Steam the salted egg yolks for 10 minutes. Leave them to cool completely, then mince them.

Heat the chicken oil in a wok and fry the curry leaves, shallots, ginger and torch ginger bud until the mixture is fragrant. Add the minced salted eggs and cook until the mixture is foamy.

Add the remaining ingredients and bring the mixture to the boil. Add the fried lobster and mix well. Serve the lobster hot, garnished with roasted shallots and chopped chives.

CRISPY FISH FILLET WITH SPICY FRISÉE SALAD

SERVES 4

Cooking oil *for deep-frying*

Bombay duck fillets *4, each about 100 g (3¹/₂ oz)*

Tapioca flour *2 Tbsp*

Sauce

Cooking oil *2 Tbsp*

Ginger *2 thin slices*

Spring onion (scallion) *1, cut into short lengths*

Coriander leaves (cilantro) *2 sprigs*

Chicken consommé (see p133) *100 ml (3¹/₃ fl oz)*

Light soy sauce *4 tsp*

Rock sugar *10 g (¹/₃ oz)*

Dark soy sauce *¹/₄ tsp*

Salad

Crispy soy bean crumb (see p141) or fried minced garlic *1 Tbsp*

Spring onion (scallion) *1, chopped*

Red chilli *1, seeded and chopped*

Salt *¹/₄ tsp*

Sesame oil *¹/₄ tsp*

Yellow frisée *a handful*

Prepare the sauce. Heat the oil in a wok and sauté the ginger and spring onion until fragrant. Add the remaining ingredients for the sauce and bring it to the boil. Remove the sauce from the heat and set it aside.

Heat the oil for deep-frying. Dust the Bombay duck fillets with tapioca flour, then deep-fry them until they are crisp and golden brown. Remove and drain well.

Prepare the salad. Mix the soy bean crumb or fried minced garlic, spring onion and red chilli with salt and sesame oil. Toss with the yellow frisée.

Serve the Bombay duck fillets with the sauce and frisée salad on the side.

FROG LEG WITH CRISPY SOY BEAN CRUMB AND ANGLED LUFFA

SERVES 4

Angled luffa *2, medium*

Cornflour (cornstarch) *for dusting*

Egg white *1, lightly beaten*

Cooking oil *1 Tbsp*

Bailing mushroom *4 thin slices*

Salt *¼ tsp*

Paste

Peeled prawns (shrimps) *160 g (5½ oz)*

Peeled water chestnuts *20 g (⅔ oz), diced*

Dried Chinese mushroom *10 g (⅓ oz), soaked to soften, stem discarded and diced*

Coriander (cilantro) stem *10 g (⅓ oz), finely chopped*

Egg white *¼*

Sugar *¼ tsp*

Salt *½ tsp*

Sesame oil *½ tsp*

Ground white pepper *⅛ tsp*

Cornflour (cornstarch) *¼ tsp*

Frog Legs

Frog legs *4*

Minced shallot *¼ tsp*

Minced ginger *¼ tsp*

Minced garlic *¼ tsp*

Minced spring onion (scallion) *¼ tsp*

Minced red chilli *¼ tsp*

Oyster sauce *¼ tsp*

Sugar *¼ tsp*

Chinese cooking wine (*hua tiao*) *¼ tsp*

Cornflour (cornstarch) *¼ tsp*

Garnish

Crispy soy bean crumb (see p141)

Black caviar

Peel the angled luffa, then cut it in half lengthwise. Using a spoon, scrape away and discard the seeds. Place the luffa in lightly salted water for about 1 minute, then drain and pat dry with paper towels. Refrigerate the poached luffa for at least 30 minutes, or until cold.

When the luffa is sufficiently chilled, prepare the paste. Chop the peeled prawns using the spine of a cleaver until the mixture is pasty. Add the remaining paste ingredients and mix well. Divide the paste into 4 portions.

Dust the inside of the chilled luffa with cornflour. Spoon a portion of the paste onto one end of a piece of luffa, then roll the luffa up. Use your fingers to keep the paste in place. Smooth some egg white over the exposed paste to smoothen the surface. Repeat to make 4 rolls.

Heat the oil in a pan and sear the luffa rolls until they are lightly brown. Remove and steam them for 3 minutes. Set the luffa rolls aside.

Sprinkle the bailing mushroom slices with salt. Using the same pan, sear the mushroom slices until they are lightly brown. Set them aside.

Combine the ingredients for the frog legs in a bowl. Mix well to marinate the frog legs.

Heat 1 Tbsp of oil in a pan. Remove the frog legs from the marinade and sear them until they are browned and cooked. Add the marinade to the pan and stir-fry lightly to coat the frog legs.

Serve the frog legs with the angled luffa and bailing mushroom. Garnish with crispy soy bean crumb and black caviar.

DEEP-FRIED AND STEAMED FISH HEAD WITH PICKLED RED CHILLIES AND SALTED BLACK BEANS

SERVES 4

Cooking oil *3 Tbsp*

Garlic *10 cloves, peeled and minced*

Song fish head *1, about 500 g*
(1 lb 1¹/₂ oz), cut into 4 pieces

Salted black beans *45 g (1¹/₂ oz)*

Chicken consommé (see p133)
100 ml (3¹/₃ fl oz)

Salt *¹/₄ tsp*

Sugar *¹/₂ tsp*

Chinese cooking wine (*hua tiao*)
¹/₄ tsp

Cornflour (cornstarch) *¹/₄ tsp, mixed
with 1 tsp water*

Chervil

Pickled Red Chillies

Red chillies *85 g (3 oz), seeded and
minced*

White vinegar *3 Tbsp*

Ginger *3 thin slices*

Salt *3 Tbsp*

Water *85 ml (2¹/₂ fl oz / ¹/₃ cup)*

Prepare the pickled red chillies. Place the red chillies, vinegar, ginger, salt and water in an airtight jar. Mix well and leave the chillies at room temperature for 3 days before storing the chillies in the refrigerator. Use the pickled red chillies as needed.

Prepare the garlic. Heat 2 Tbsp of oil and fry the minced garlic until it is light golden brown. Remove and drain well.

Place the fish head, black beans, roasted garlic and pickled red chillies into 4 heatproof (flameproof) bowls.

Heat the remaining oil in a wok and add the chicken consommé, salt, sugar and cooking wine. Bring the mixture to the boil and stir in the cornflour mixture to thicken the sauce.

Pour the sauce over the fish head and steam for about 10 minutes, or until the fish head is cooked. Garnish the fish head with chervil and serve hot.

Meat and Poulty

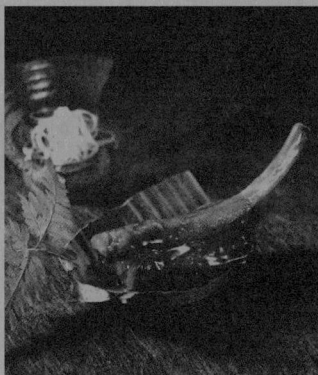

SERVES 4

Beef tenderloin *200 g (7 oz)*

Cooking oil *1 Tbsp*

Fresh lily bulbs *40 g (1¹/₂ oz),*
blanched; petals separated

Marinade
Cooking oil *1 Tbsp*

Garlic *6 cloves, peeled*

Coffee powder *3 Tbsp*

Vanilla pods *2, split and seeds*
scraped out

Shallot oil *6 Tbsp*

Ground black pepper *¹/₄ tsp*

Salt *¹/₈ tsp*

Sauce Jelly
Chicken consommé *(see p133)*
3 Tbsp

Chinese wolfberries *1 tsp*

Red wine *2 tsp*

Salt *¹/₈ tsp*

Gelatine powder *¹/₈ tsp*

Garnish
Seaweed powder *(see p138)*

COFFEE BEEF TENDERLOIN
WITH SAUTÉED FRESH LILY BULB

Prepare this dish a day ahead.

Prepare the marinade. Heat the oil and fry the garlic until they are light golden brown and fragrant. Drain and place the garlic in a bowl with the remaining marinade ingredients. Add the beef and leave it to marinate in the refrigerator overnight.

Heat a pan with 1 Tbsp of oil and sear the marinated beef until medium or cooked to your preference. Set aside and keep the beef warm.

Combine the ingredients for the sauce jelly except the gelatine powder, in a small pot. Simmer the sauce over low heat for about 10 minutes, then stir in the gelatine powder. Remove the sauce from the heat and refrigerate it for about 10 minutes, or until the sauce is set. Chop the sauce into small cubes and spoon them onto the lily buds. Sprinkle with seaweed powder.

Slice the beef into 4 portions and serve with the lily buds and sauce jelly.

ROAST SUCKLING PIG SKIN WITH SEARED FOIE GRAS AND CHEESE CRACKER

SERVES 4

Foie gras *150 g (5¹/₃ oz), diced*

Salt *¹/₄ tsp*

Plain (all-purpose) flour *50 g (1¹/₂ oz)*

Cooking oil *1 Tbsp*

Parmesan cheese *100 g (3¹/₂ oz), grated*

Suckling pig skin *4 small square pieces*

Sauce

Yellow miso paste *2 tsp*

Salted bean paste *2 tsp*

Sugar *3 tsp*

Oyster sauce *1 tsp*

Light soy sauce *1 tsp*

Sesame oil *1 tsp*

Chicken consommé (see p133) *3 Tbsp*

Cooking oil *¹/₂ Tbsp*

Garnish
Yellow frisée

Sprinkle the diced foie gras with salt, then dust with plain flour. Heat the oil in a pan and sear the foie gras pieces until they are brown on all sides.

Prepare the cheese cracker. Place a non-stick pan over low heat and sprinkle the Parmesan cheese into the pan. Leave it for about 30 seconds, or until the cheese is melted and bubbling. Peel and remove the melted cheese from the pan. Leave it to cool on a sheet of greaseproof paper. When the cheese cracker is cool, break it up into small pieces and top each piece with some foie gras. Garnish them with chives and place on a serving plate.

Combine the ingredients for the sauce, except the cooking oil. Heat the oil in a wok and add the sauce until it is heated through.

Serve the suckling pig skin on a bed of frisée leaves with the sauce. Serve with the foie gras on the cheese crackers.

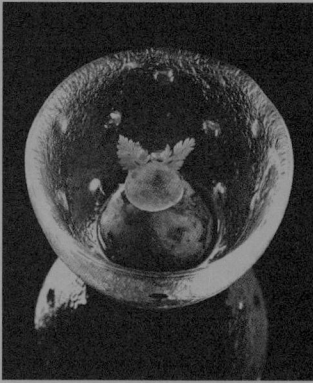

SERVES 4

Lion's Head

Minced pork belly *200 g (7 oz)*

Pork fat *40 g (1¹/₂ oz), minced*

Shiitake mushrooms *40 g (1¹/₂ oz), caps wiped, stems discarded, and minced*

Water chestnuts *4, peeled and chopped*

Coriander (cilantro) stems *2*

Dried mandarin peel *1 small piece, soaked and minced*

Cornflour (cornstarch) *1 tsp*

Seasoning

Egg white *1*

Light soy sauce *3 tsp*

Sugar *3 tsp*

Ground white pepper *¹/₂ tsp*

Chinese cooking wine (*hua tiao*) *3 Tbsp*

Chicken consommé (see p133) *625 ml (20 fl oz / 2¹/₂ cups)*

Sauce

Cooking oil *¹/₂ Tbsp*

Ginger *2 slices*

Spring onion (scallion) *1, cut into short lengths*

Coriander leaves (cilantro) *2 sprigs*

Chicken consommé (see p133) *100 ml (3¹/₃ fl oz)*

Light soy sauce *1 Tbsp*

Rock sugar *10 g (¹/₃ oz)*

Dark soy sauce *¹/₈ tsp*

Garnish

Salted egg yolk *1*

Cooking oil

Chopped chives

Chervil

STEAMED LION'S HEAD

Combine the ingredients for the lion's head and the seasoning and mix well. Divide the mixture into 4 portions and roll each portion into a ball.

Steam the meatballs for 5 minutes. Heat 1 Tbsp of oil in a wok and sear the steamed meatballs until they are lightly browned. Transfer the meatballs to serving bowls.

Prepare the sauce. Heat the oil in a wok and sauté the ginger and spring onion until fragrant. Add the remaining ingredients for the sauce and mix well. When the sauce is heated through, pour it over the meatballs.

Prepare the garnish. Rub the salted egg yolk with a little oil, then use a cleaver to smash the egg yolk into a thin sheet, on a plastic chopping board. Using a small ring cutter, cut out 4 rounds of egg yolk, then steam the egg yolk rounds for about 20 seconds.

Top the meatballs with the steamed salted egg yolk rounds and serve garnished with chives and chervil.

BRAISED PORK RIB IN SWEET AND SOUR SAUCE

SERVES 4

Pork ribs *4, each about 100 g (3¹/₂ oz), parboiled*

Cooking oil *for deep-frying*

Egg yolk *¹/₂, beaten*

Cornflour (cornstarch) *4 Tbsp*

Marinade

Chicken consommé (see p133)
2 litres (64 fl oz / 8 cups)

Rock sugar *30 g (1 oz)*

Light soy sauce *10 g (¹/₃ oz)*

Oyster sauce *30 g (1 oz)*

Chinese cooking wine (*hua tiao*)
2 Tbsp

Black glutinous rice *20 g (²/₃ oz)*

Bay leaves *2*

Dried chilli *1*

Sweet and Sour Sauce

Water *100 ml (3¹/₃ fl oz)*

Sugar *120 g (4¹/₂ oz)*

Salt *¹/₂ tsp*

Brown sugar *20 g (²/₃ oz)*

White vinegar *3 Tbsp*

Sweet chilli sauce *4 Tbsp*

Tomato sauce *4 Tbsp*

Garnish

Orange zest

Combine the ingredients for the marinade in a pot. Add the pork ribs, cover and simmer over low heat for about 1 hour, or until the ribs are tender. Remove the ribs and discard the marinade.

Heat the oil for deep-frying. Dip the ribs into the egg yolk, then coat them with cornflour and deep-fry until golden brown. Drain well and set aside.

Combine the ingredients for the sweet and sour sauce in a wok and cook it over low heat until the sauce is just heated through. Add the deep-fried pork ribs and mix to coat well. Serve the ribs garnished with orange zest.

SEARED FOIE GRAS WITH CARAMELISED APPLE

SERVES 4

Seared Foie Gras

Foie gras *4 slices, each about 60 g (2 oz)*

Salt *¹/₈ tsp*

Ground black pepper *¹/₈ tsp*

Paprika *¹/₈ tsp*

Tempura flour *¹/₈ tsp*

Cooking oil *1 Tbsp*

Caramelised Apple

Green apples *2*

Cooking oil *1 Tbsp*

Tempura flour *¹/₈ tsp*

Butter *¹/₂ tsp*

Honey *2 tsp*

Salt *¹/₈ tsp*

Rum *2 tsp*

Sauce

Rosella flowers *6*

Red wine *150 ml (5 fl oz)*

Chicken consommé (see p133) *80 ml (2¹/₂ fl oz)*

Honey *2 Tbsp*

Bay leaves *2*

Chinese wolfberries *2 Tbsp*

Raisins *2 Tbsp*

Combine the ingredients for the sauce in a pot and cook over low heat, stirring, until the sauce is reduced and thick. Strain the sauce and set it aside. Reserve the rosella flowers for garnish.

Dust the foie gras with salt, pepper, paprika and tempura flour.

Heat the oil in a wok and sear the dusted foie gras until they are light brown on both sides. Set aside.

Peel the apples and cut each one into 6 wedges. Remove the seeds and smoothen the edges of each apple wedge with a small paring knife.

Heat the oil in a wok. Dust the apples with tempura flour, then pan-sear them until lightly brown on all sides. Add the butter, honey, salt and rum and tilt the wok around until the apple wedges are well-coated with the sauce.

Place 3 apple wedges on each plate and top with a slice of foie gras. Drizzle with sauce and garnish with rosella flowers. Serve immediately.

SEARED FOIE GRAS WITH CARAMELISED STRAWBERRY AND PEKING DUCK SKIN WITH CURRY-MAYO PRAWN

SERVES 4

Butter *1/2 tsp*

Strawberries *4, washed and left whole*

Plain (all-purpose) flour *for coating*

Honey *1 tsp*

Salt *3/8 tsp*

Brandy *1/2 tsp*

Cooking oil *1 Tbsp*

Foie gras *4 small pieces, each about 60 g (2 oz)*

Peking duck skin *4 small slices*

Prawns (shrimps) *4, medium, peeled*

Sesame oil *1/8 tsp*

Egg white *1/2*

Curry-Mayo Sauce

Mayonnaise *6 tsp*

Sweetened condensed milk *3 tsp*

Curry powder *1 tsp*

Lemon juice *1 tsp*

Garnish

White sesame seeds *1 tsp, roasted*

Chervil

Black caviar

Heat the butter in a pan. Dust the strawberries lightly with flour and sear them until they are golden brown. This takes about 1 minute. Add the honey, *1/8* tsp of salt and brandy to glaze the strawberries. Remove the strawberries from the pan and cut the caps off the strawberries. Set the strawberries and their caps aside.

Heat the oil in a clean pan. Rub the foie gras with *1/8* tsp of salt and dust lightly with some plain flour. Sear the foie gras until lightly browned. Sandwich each foie gras piece between a strawberry and a piece of duck skin.

Combine the ingredients for the curry-mayo sauce and refrigerate it until cold. This will take about 30 minutes.

When the sauce is sufficiently chilled, heat the oil for deep-frying.

Marinate the prawns with *1/8* tsp of salt, sesame oil and egg white, then coat them with some plain flour. Deep-fry the prawns until they are golden brown, then drain and toss with chilled curry-mayo sauce. Sprinkle with sesame seeds and garnish with caviar and chervil. Serve immediately with the foie gras and strawberries.

SEARED WAGYU BEEF WITH ASSORTED SALAD GREENS IN CRISPY CHEESE BASKET

SERVES 4

Wagyu beef fillet *320 g (11¹/2 oz),*
trimmed

Salt *¹/2 tsp*

Ground black pepper *¹/4 tsp*

Cooking oil *1 Tbsp*

Assorted salad greens

Crispy Cheese Basket

Parmesan cheese *200 g (7 oz),*
grated

Walnut Dressing

Walnut oil *4 Tbsp*

Salt *¹/4 tsp*

Sugar *¹/4 tsp*

White vinegar *¹/4 tsp*

Lemon juice *¹/4 tsp*

Garnish

Salted egg yolks *2*

Chopped chives

Sprinkle the beef fillet with salt and pepper. Heat the oil in a pan and sear the beef to your preferred doneness. Cut the beef into 4 equal pieces and set aside.

Prepare the garnish. Steam the salted egg yolks for 10 minutes, then leave them to cool completely. Mince the cooled egg yolks and sprinkle over the beef. Garnish the beef with chives.

Prepare the cheese basket. Heat a non-stick pan and sprinkle in one-quarter of the cheese until the cheese is melted and bubbly. Peel off the cheese and place it over a small, overturned mould. Leave it to cool. Repeat this step to make 3 more cheese baskets.

Prepare the walnut dressing. Blend (process) the walnut oil, then add the remaining ingredients. Blend to mix well, then toss with the salad greens.

Serve the beef with the mixed salad greens in a cheese basket.

SHANGHAINESE GLASS NOODLES WITH ROASTED LEMON GRASS CHICKEN

Boneless chicken drumsticks 2

Shanghainese glass noodles 120 g (4¹/₂ oz)

Marinade

Lemon grass 2 stalks, ends trimmed, hard outer leaves removed

Dark soy sauce 2 tsp

Oyster sauce 4 tsp

Light soy sauce 2 tsp

Fish sauce ¹/₂ tsp

Cooking oil 2 tsp

Water 4 Tbsp

Sauce

Sesame oil 1 tsp

Chilli oil ¹/₄ tsp

Salt 1 tsp

Honey ¹/₂ tsp

Plum sauce ¹/₂ tsp

Lemon juice ¹/₂ tsp

Garnish

White sesame seeds

Chervil

Prepare this dish at least 3–4 hours ahead.

Prepare the marinade. Use only the bottom 5 cm (2 in) of the lemon grass stalks and mince them finely. Place the lemon grass into a pot and add the remaining ingredients for the marinade. Bring the mixture to the boil over medium heat, then remove it from the heat and cover the pot. Leave the marinade covered until it is completely cool.

Place the chicken drumsticks into the cooled marinade and place the pot into the refrigerator for 3–4 hours or overnight.

Preheat the oven to 220°C (440°F). Remove the chicken drumsticks from the marinade and brush them lightly with oil. Place the chicken drumsticks in a roasting pan and roast them in the oven for 12–15 minutes, or until they are just cooked. Reserve the chicken juices in the pan.

Blanch the glass noodles for 2 minutes until softened, then plunge them into cold water. Drain well.

Combine the ingredients for the sauce and add some of the chicken juices from the roasting pan. Toss the glass noodles in the sauce.

Slice the chicken and serve with the noodles. Garnish with sesame seeds and chervil.

NOTE The excess roasting juices in the roasting pan can be used as a dipping sauce for the chicken.

SEARED DUCK BREAST AND FOIE GRAS WITH SAUTÉED POTATOES IN HOISIN SAUCE

SERVES 4

Duck breast *1, about 200 g (7 oz)*

Salt

Ground black pepper *1/4 tsp*

Cooking oil *for deep-frying*

Foie gras *40 g (1 1/2 oz), cut into small cubes*

Plain (all-purpose) flour *1 tsp*

Baby potatoes *2, scrubbed clean and cut into cubes*

Finely chopped black truffle *1/2 tsp*

Chopped chives *1/2 tsp*

Gelatine powder *1/8 tsp*

Sauce

Cooking oil *1 Tbsp*

Minced garlic *1/4 tsp*

Minced ginger *1/4 tsp*

Minced shallots *1/4 tsp*

Hoisin sauce *2 tsp*

Sugar *1/4 tsp*

Oyster sauce *1/4 tsp*

Hot bean paste *1/4 tsp*

Chicken consommé (see p133) *80 ml (2 1/2 fl oz / 1/3 cup)*

Chinese cooking wine (*hua tiao*) *1 tsp*

Cornflour (cornstarch) *1/2 tsp, mixed with 1 tsp water*

Season the duck breast with 1/8 tsp of salt and pepper. Heat 1 Tbsp of oil in a wok, then sear the seasoned duck breast until it is cooked medium-well. Cut the duck breast into 4 slices and set aside.

Season the foie gras cubes with 1/8 tsp of salt, then dust lightly with plain flour. Using a clean pan, heat 1 Tbsp of oil and sear the foie gras. Set the foie gras aside.

Heat the oil for deep-frying and deep-fry the potato cubes until they are crisp and golden brown. Drain well, then toss them with the finely chopped truffle, chives and 1/8 tsp of salt. Toss again, this time with the seared foie gras and divide the mixture into 4 portions. Spoon each portion onto a serving plate and arrange a slice of duck on top.

Prepare the sauce. Heat the oil and sauté the minced garlic, ginger and shallots until they are fragrant. Add the remaining ingredients for the sauce except the cornflour mixture and bring it to the boil. Taste the sauce and adjust with salt if necessary. Stir in the cornflour mixture to thicken the sauce.

Spoon 5 tsp of sauce into a small bowl and stir in the gelatine powder. Refrigerate the sauce for about 10 minutes until it sets. Chop the sauce jelly up finely and spoon it on top of the duck. Serve this dish cold.

BRAISED OX TAIL WITH RADISH

SERVES 4

Cooking oil *1 Tbsp*

Ox tail *480 g (1 lb 1 oz), cut into 4 pieces*

Salt *¹/₂ tsp*

Plain (all-purpose) flour *3 tsp*

Cornflour (cornstarch) *¹/₂ tsp, mixed with 1 tsp water*

Sauce
Chicken consommé (see p133)
 1 litre (32 fl oz / 4 cups)

Fermented bean curd (*lam yu*)
 ¹/₂ tsp

Salted bean paste *¹/₄ tsp*

Oyster sauce *¹/₄ tsp*

Light soy sauce *¹/₄ tsp*

Rock sugar *30 g (1 oz)*

Chinese cooking wine (*hua tiao*)
 3 Tbsp

Red dates *5*

White radish (daikon) *200 g (7 oz), peeled and cut into 2.5-cm (1-in) rounds*

Spring onion (scallion) *1, cut into short lengths*

Ginger *2.5-cm (1-in) knob, peeled and diced*

Carrot *50 g (2 oz), peeled and diced*

GARNISH
Alfalfa sprouts

Heat the oil in a pan. Rub the ox tail with salt, then dust with the plain flour and sear lightly.

Combine the ingredients for the sauce in a pot and add the seared ox tail. Cover the pot and simmer over low heat for about 30 minutes.

Remove the radish rounds from the pot and place them in a steamer. Steam the radish for about 30 minutes, or until they are tender.

Remove the ox tail and set it aside on a serving plate.

Strain the sauce into a wok and simmer it over low heat until it is just bubbling. Stir in the cornflour mixture to thicken the sauce.

Drizzle the sauce over the ox tail and serve it with the steamed radish on the side. Garnish with alfalfa sprouts.

STEWED BEEF CHEEK
WITH YOUNG GARLIC

SERVES 4

Cooking oil *2 Tbsp*

Beef cheek *320 g (11¹/₂ oz)*

Salt *¹/₂ tsp*

Plain (all-purpose) flour *3 tsp*

Garlic *12 cloves, peeled*

Sauce

Chicken consommé (see p133)
1 litre (32 fl oz / 4 cups)

White miso paste *¹/₄ tsp*

Oyster sauce *¹/₄ tsp*

Light soy sauce *¹/₄ tsp*

Rock sugar *30 g (1 oz)*

Chinese cooking wine (*hua tiao*)
3 Tbsp

Red dates *8*

Star anise *1*

Dried mandarin peel *1 small piece*

White radish (daikon) *100 g (3¹/₂ oz),
peeled and diced*

Spring onion (scallion) *1, cut into
short lengths*

Ginger *2.5-cm (1-in) knob, peeled and
smashed*

Carrot *50 g (2 oz), peeled and diced*

Cornflour (cornstarch) *1¹/₂ tsp, mixed
with 3 tsp water*

Garnish

Chinese wolfberries *1 tsp, soaked for
15 minutes and split*

Chervil

Heat 1 Tbsp of oil in a pan. Dust the beef cheek with salt and plain flour, then sear it lightly.

Using a clean pan, roast the garlic until light golden brown and fragrant. Set the garlic aside.

Place the ingredients for the sauce, except the cornflour, in a pot. Add the seared beef, cover the pot and simmer over low heat for 30 minutes, then place the pot in a steamer and steam for 30 minutes, or until the beef is tender. Remove the beef and cut it into 4 portions. Set aside and keep the beef warm.

Strain the sauce into a wok. Add the roasted garlic and simmer the sauce over low heat until it is just bubbling. Stir in the cornflour mixture to thicken the sauce.

Drizzle the sauce over the beef and serve, garnished with the roasted garlic, wolfberries and chervil.

Vegetables and Mushrooms

DEEP-FRIED BEAN CURD, PRAWN AND SPINACH BALL COATED WITH BREAD CUBES

SERVES 4

Silken bean curd *150 g (5¹/₃ oz)*

Prawns (shrimps) *80 g (3 oz), peeled*

Spinach leaves *40 g (1¹/₂ oz),*
  blanched and chopped

Cheddar cheese *4 square pieces,*
  each about 20 g (²/₃ oz)

Cooking oil *for deep-frying*

White bread *100 g (3¹/₂ oz), crust*
  removed and cut into small cubes

Seasoning

Salt *¹/₄ tsp*

Sugar *¹/₂ tsp*

Sesame oil *¹/₂ tsp*

Egg white *¹/₂*

Cornflour (cornstarch) *¹/₄ tsp*

Ground white pepper *¹/₈ tsp*

Cut the bean curd into small pieces, then press it through a fine mesh sieve into a bowl. Chop the prawns up using the spine of a cleaver until the mixture is pasty.

Combine the bean curd, prawns, spinach and ingredients for the seasoning in a small bowl. Divide the mixture into 4 portions and roll each portion into a ball. Press a cheddar cheese square into each ball and roll the balls again to enclose the cheese.

Heat the oil for deep-frying. Coat the balls with the bread cubes and deep-fry them over medium heat until they are golden brown and crisp. This takes about 3 minutes. Drain well and serve hot.

STEAMED ASSORTED MUSHROOMS IN MUI CHOY LEAVES

SERVES 4

Preserved mustard cabbage (*mui choy*) leaves *4, soaked overnight*

Cooking oil *1 Tbsp*

Garlic *4, peeled*

Dried morel mushrooms *60 g (2 oz), soaked overnight and steamed for 10 minutes*

White hon shimeji mushrooms *60 g (2 oz)*

Brown hon shimeji mushrooms *60 g (2 oz)*

Bailing mushroom *60 g (2 oz), diced*

Prepared dried scallops (see p148) *4*

Cornflour (cornstarch) *1/2 tsp, mixed with 1 tsp water*

Balsamic Vinegar Reduction

Balsamic vinegar *200 ml (6 1/2 fl oz)*

Ginger *1 slice*

Brown sugar *2 tsp*

Seasoning

Chicken consommé (see p133) *3 Tbsp*

Oyster sauce *1/4 tsp*

Sugar *1/4 tsp*

Chinese cooking wine (*hua tiao*) *1/2 tsp*

Garnish

Black truffle slices

Chervil

Prepare the balsamic vinegar reduction. Combine the balsamic vinegar, ginger and sugar in a pan and simmer over low heat until the liquid is reduced to about 4 Tbsp. This takes about 45 minutes. Set the reduction aside.

Drain the soaked mustard cabbage leaves, then blanch them in lightly salted water. Pat the leaves dry and refrigerate them until they are cold.

Heat the oil in a wok and fry the garlic until they are light golden brown. Add all the mushrooms and prepared scallops, and stir-fry until the mixture is fragrant.

Add the ingredients for the seasoning and stir in the cornflour mixture to thicken the sauce. Remove the mixture from the heat and leave it to cool to room temperature before refrigerating it for about 30 minutes, or until it is cold.

Line 4 small heatproof (flameproof) moulds with the chilled mustard cabbage leaves, leaving the edges of the leaves hanging over the mould. Spoon the chilled mushroom mixture into the moulds, then enclose the filling with the leaves. Steam the moulds for 5 minutes until they are heated through.

Turn the moulds upside down on serving plates to tip the steamed mushroom bundle out. Garnish with truffle and chervil and serve with balsamic vinegar reduction.

SICHUAN-STYLE WOK-FRIED SHISHITO PEPPER WITH DRIED PRAWNS

SERVES 4

Cooking oil

Shishito peppers (Japanese green chillies) *4, small*

Dried prawns (shrimps) *50 g (2 oz), rinsed and drained*

Salted black beans *10 g (¹/₃ oz)*

Spring onion (scallion) *10 g (¹/₃ oz), trimmed and chopped*

Ginger *10 g (¹/₃ oz), peeled and chopped*

Garlic *10 g (¹/₃ oz), peeled and chopped*

Sichuan pickled vegetable *10 g (¹/₃ oz), soaked for 1 hour, rinsed and chopped*

Seasoning

Chicken consommé (see p133) *2 Tbsp*

Oyster sauce *¹/₄ tsp*

Hot bean paste *¹/₄ tsp*

White miso paste *¹/₈ tsp*

Sugar *¹/₄ tsp*

Chinese cooking wine (*hua tiao*) *¹/₂ tsp*

Cornflour (cornstarch) *¹/₂ tsp, mixed with 1 tsp water*

Garnish

Red shiso cress

Seaweed powder (see p138)

Heat ¹/₂ Tbsp of oil in a wok and sear the shishito peppers lightly. Remove from the heat and set aside.

Heat another ¹/₂ Tbsp oil in the same wok and fry the dried prawns until they are fragrant and golden brown. Add the salted black beans, spring onion, ginger, garlic and Sichuan pickled vegetable and stir-fry lightly.

Add the ingredients for the seasoning, except the cornflour mixture, and the seared shishito peppers. Stir in the cornflour mixture to thicken the sauce.

Dish out onto a serving plate and garnish with shiso cress and seaweed powder. Serve hot.

POACHED CHINESE CABBAGE
WITH SALTED EGG CREAM SAUCE

SERVES 4

Chinese (napa) cabbage *4 small heads*

Chicken consommé (see p133)
500 ml (16 fl oz / 4 cups)

Salt *1 tsp*

Sugar *1 tsp*

Chinese cooking wine (*hua tiao*)
1 tsp

Sauce

Salted egg yolks *4*

Chicken oil* *2 tsp*

Chicken consommé (see p133)
300 ml (10 fl oz / 1¹/₄ cups)

Salt *¹/₄ tsp*

Sugar *¹/₄ tsp*

Chinese cooking wine (*hua tiao*)
¹/₂ tsp

White peppercorns *5*

Cornflour (cornstarch) *¹/₄ tsp*

Garnish
Chinese wolfberries *1 tsp, soaked for
15 minutes and drained*

Chervil

Remove the large outer leaves of each head of cabbage (about 6 layers) to get to the heart. Refrigerate the large leaves for use in other recipes. Blanch the cabbage hearts for about 2 minutes, then drain well.

Bring the chicken consommé to the boil and season it with salt, sugar and cooking wine. Add the blanched cabbage hearts and simmer over low heat for about 4 minutes. Drain and set aside.

Steam the salted egg yolks for about 10 minutes, then leave them to cool completely, before mincing.

Heat the chicken oil in a wok and add the minced egg yolk. Cook until the mixture becomes foamy. Add the chicken consommé, salt, sugar, cooking wine and peppercorns and bring the mixture to the boil. Stir in the cornflour mixture to thicken the sauce, then remove it from the heat.

Garnish the cabbage with the wolfberries and chervil. Serve with the salted egg cream sauce.

*CHICKEN OIL

MAKES ABOUT 2 TBSP

Cooking oil *1 Tbsp*

Ginger *2.5-cm (1-in) knob, peeled
and minced*

Spring onion (scallion) *1*

Chicken fat *100 g (3¹/₂ oz)*

Heat the oil in a wok and sear the ginger and spring onion until fragrant. Add the chicken fat and cook it over low heat until the fat is rendered. Strain the oil and store it in an airtight container at room temperature for up to 1 week.

PAN-SEARED WHOLE MUSHROOM WITH ASSORTED GREENS AND WALNUT DRESSING

SERVES 4

Fresh whole mushrooms (any kind)
 4, large

Cooking oil *1 Tbsp*

Salt *1/8 tsp*

Assorted salad greens

Chinese wolfberries *1 tsp, soaked
 for 30 minutes and drained*

Stock
Lean pork *250 g (9 oz), poached*

Chicken feet *120 g (41/2 oz), poached*

Chicken *250 g (9 oz), poached*

Chicken consommé *(see p133)
 500 ml (16 fl oz / 2 cups)*

Rock sugar *40 g (11/2 oz)*

Oyster sauce *2 tsp*

Dark soy sauce *1 tsp*

Walnut Dressing
Walnut oil *4 Tbsp*

Salt *1/4 tsp*

Sugar *1/4 tsp*

White vinegar *1/4 tsp*

Lemon juice *1/4 tsp*

Combine the ingredients for the stock in a pot and bring to the boil. Add the mushrooms and simmer over low heat for about 30 minutes, or until the liquid almost completely evaporates. Set aside the mushrooms and discard all the other ingredients.

Heat the oil and sear the mushrooms until they are lightly browned. Season them with salt.

Prepare the walnut dressing. Place the walnut oil in a food blender (processor) and blend, then add the remaining ingredients and blend again to create a dressing. Toss the salad greens with the dressing and garnish with wolfberries.

Serve the mushrooms with the tossed salad greens on the side.

Rice and Noodles

SERVES 4

BRAISED MEE POK WITH CLAMS AND WHITE HON SHIMEJI MUSHROOMS IN XO SAUCE

Mee pok (flat yellow noodles) *200 g (7 oz)*

Cooking oil *1 Tbsp*

Dried sole powder (see Note) *¼ tsp*

Garlic *15 cloves, peeled*

Clams (with shell) *320 g (11½ oz)*

White hon shimeji mushrooms *200 g (7 oz)*

Sauce

Chicken consommé (see p133) *800 ml (26 fl oz / 3¼ cups)*

Oyster sauce *2 tsp*

XO sauce *2 tsp*

Sugar *1 tsp*

Ground white pepper *⅛ tsp*

Dark soy sauce *¼ tsp*

Bring a pot of water to the boil and blanch the noodles for about 20 seconds. Remove the noodles using a wire strainer, then plunge the noodles immediately into a basin of cold water. Drain and set the noodles aside.

Heat the oil in a wok and sauté the dried sole powder until fragrant. Add the garlic, clams and hon shimeji mushrooms and sauté until fragrant. Remove and discard any clams that do not open.

Add the ingredients for the sauce to the wok, then add the noodles. Allow the noodles to simmer for about 1 minute, or until the noodles absorb the sauce and the dish is almost dry. Serve the noodles immediately.

NOTE To prepare dried sole powder, deep-fry dried sole over low heat until crisp and golden. This takes about 2 minutes. Drain the sole well and leave to cool. Blend (process) the cooled sole into powder and store in an airtight container at room temperature for up to 1 month.

LA MIAN AND SEARED SRI LANKAN CRAB CLAW IN SUPERIOR CHICKEN CONSOMMÉ

SERVES 4

Sri Lankan crab claws *4*

Salt *¹/₈ tsp*

Dried *la mian* sticks *200 g (7 oz)*

Superior chicken consommé
  (see p145) *300 ml (10 fl oz /
  1¹/₄ cups)*

Garnish

Black ebiko

Red ebiko

Chives

Crack the crab claw shells and sprinkle them with salt. Steam the crab claws for about 4 minutes, or until the shells change colour and the crab is cooked.

Divide the *la mian* sticks into 2 equal bundles and tie both ends of each bundle with kitchen string to keep the *la mian* together. Bring a pot of water to the boil and blanch the *la mian* until soft.

Cut each bundle of *la mian* in half, then steam the bundles for 1 minute. Remove the string and place the *la mian* on deep serving plates.

Place a crab claw on each plate, then ladle the superior chicken consommé around the *la mian* and crab claws. Serve immediately, garnished with black and red ebiko and chives.

WARM GLUTINOUS RICE WITH LOTUS SEEDS ON ORANGE JUICE-MARINATED LOTUS ROOT SLICE

SERVES 4

Glutinous rice 120 g (4½ oz), soaked overnight

Cooking oil 2 Tbsp

Dried prawns (shrimps) 20 g (⅔ oz), rinsed and minced

Shiitake mushrooms 20 g (⅔ oz), caps wiped and diced

Hon shimeji mushrooms 20 g (⅔ oz)

Seasoning
Light soy sauce ¼ tsp

Oyster sauce ½ tsp

Sugar ¼ tsp

Sesame oil ¼ tsp

Dark soy sauce ¼ tsp

Ground white pepper ¼ tsp

Marinated Lotus Root
Freshly squeezed orange juice 100 ml (3⅓ fl oz)

Freshly squeezed lemon juice 3 Tbsp

Salted plums 3

Salt ¼ tsp

Lotus root 8 slices

Fried Lotus Seeds
Cooking oil for deep-frying

Lotus seeds 4

Plain (all-purpose) flour for coating

Garnish
Seaweed powder (see p138)

Prepare this dish a day ahead.

Prepare the marinated lotus root. Bring the juices, salted plums and salt to the boil in a small pot. Remove the pot from the heat and add the lotus root slices. Leave the pot to cool before refrigerating it overnight.

Drain the soaked rice and steam for 30–40 minutes, or until the rice is tender, but still firm to the bite.

Heat the oil in a wok and sauté the minced dried prawns until fragrant and lightly browned. Add the mushrooms and steamed glutinous rice and sauté lightly. Add the seasoning and mix well.

Prepare the lotus seeds for garnish. Heat enough oil for deep-frying in a small pot. Coat the lotus seeds with plain flour and deep-fry until golden brown. Drain well.

Remove the lotus root from the marinade and arrange them on serving plates, topped with a small spoonful of glutinous rice. Garnish with lotus seeds and seaweed powder before serving.

Dried *la mian* sticks *200 g (7 oz)*

Consommé
Dashi* *3 Tbsp*
Japanese soy sauce *4 tsp*
Mirin *4 tsp*
Sugar *1/2 tsp*

Garnish
Black caviar
Chives
Orange zest
Roasted white sesame seeds

MAKES ABOUT 2.5 LITRES
(80 FL OZ / 10 CUPS)

Bonito flakes *50 g (2 oz)*
Konbu (dried kelp) *1 tsp*
Water *3 litres (96 fl oz / 6 cups)*

CHILLED LA MIAN

Bring a pot of water to the boil and blanch the *la mian* for about 2 minutes until the noodles are soft. Drain and plunge the *la mian* immediately into cold water. Refrigerate until the *la mian* is cold.

Combine the ingredients for the consommé in a small pot and bring it to the boil. Leave the consommmé to cool before refrigerating it until it is cold. Serve the consommé on the side with the *la mian*. Garnish with caviar, chives, orange zest and sesame seeds.

*DASHI

Combine all the ingredients in a pot and bring to the boil, then lower heat and simmer the stock over low heat for 30 minutes. Strain and use as needed.

CRISPY EGG NOODLES AND LARGE CLAMS IN CHICKEN CONSOMMÉ

SERVES 4

Egg noodles *200 g (7 oz)*

Cooking oil *for deep-frying*

Large clams (with shell) *4*

Minced ginger *¹/₄ tsp*

Minced garlic *¹/₄ tsp*

Cornflour (cornstarch) *2 tsp, mixed with 4 tsp water*

Egg yolks *2, lightly beaten*

Seasoning

Chicken consommé (see p133) *300 ml (10 fl oz / 3¹/₄ cups)*

Oyster sauce *1 tsp*

Sugar *1 tsp*

Chinese cooking wine (*hua tiao*) *2 tsp*

Ground white pepper *¹/₈ tsp*

Garnish

Chopped chives

Bring a pot of water to the boil and blanch the noodles until they are soft. Plunge the noodles immediately into a basin of cold water, then drain them and place them in a colander to drain until completely dry.

Heat the oil in a deep pan and add the drained noodles. The oil should just cover the noodles. Leave the noodles in the hot oil for 2 minutes, or until the noodles are crisp and golden brown. Remove the noodles and drain well.

Steam the clams for 5 minutes. Remove the clams from their shells, then clean the shells for use as plates for serving the noodles in. Divide the noodles into 4 portions and place each portion on a shell.

Heat 1 Tbsp of oil in a wok. Add the minced ginger and garlic and sauté until fragrant. Add the seasoning and bring the mixture to the boil. Add the clam meat and stir in the cornflour mixture to thicken the sauce.

Add the lightly beaten egg yolks and remove sauce from the heat. Pour the sauce over the noodles, then place a clam on top of each portion of noodles. Garnish with chives and serve immediately.

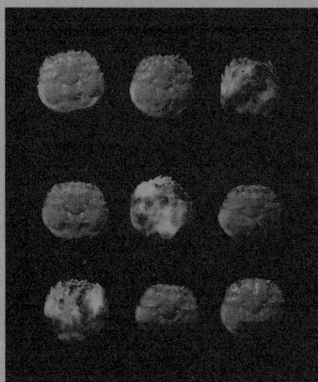

BAKED RICE WITH CRABMEAT AND CHEESE

SERVES 4

Hairy or flower crabs *4, cleaned*

Cooking oil *3 Tbsp*

Egg whites *4, lightly beaten*

Steamed white rice *400 g (14¹/₃ oz),
refrigerated overnight*

Thai asparagus *30 g (1 oz), blanched
and cut into small cubes*

Carrot *30 g (1 oz), peeled, blanched
and cut into small cubes*

Salt *1 tsp*

Sugar *¹/₂ tsp*

Ground white pepper *¹/₈ tsp*

Parmesan cheese *100 g (3¹/₃ oz),
grated*

Chinese (Yunnan) ham *40 g (1¹/₂ oz),
minced*

Steam the crabs for 5 minutes, then remove and set the crabmeat aside. Clean the shells and reserve them to serve the rice in.

Heat the oil in a wok and add the egg whites. Stir-fry the egg whites until fragrant, then add the steamed rice, crabmeat, asparagus, carrot, salt, sugar and pepper. Cook until the rice is fragrant. Remove the rice from the heat and pack the hot rice into the cleaned crab shells.

Combine the cheese and ham and sprinkle over the rice. Place the filled crab shells on a baking tray and place under a salamander for 20 seconds until lightly browned. Alternatively, place the crab shells in an oven preheated to 180°C (350°F) until the cheese is lightly browned. Remove and serve hot.

BRAISED BEEF CONSOMMÉ LA MIAN

SERVES 4

Dried *la mian* sticks *200 g (7 oz)*

Cornflour (cornstarch) *1 tsp*

Beef Consommé

Beef (muscle) *1 kg (2 lb 3 oz), parboiled*

Chicken consommé (see p133) *2 litres (64 fl oz / 8 cups)*

Coriander (cilantro) roots *2*

Chinese celery *2 stalks*

Pickled garlic *50 g (2 oz)*

Star anise *4*

Cinnamon sticks *2*

Cloves *10*

Seasoning

Rock sugar *1 Tbsp*

Fish sauce *4 Tbsp*

Dark soy sauce *¹⁄₂ Tbsp*

Garlic oil *1 Tbsp*

Ground white pepper *¹⁄₈ tsp*

Garnish

Seaweed powder (see p138)

Bring a pot of water to the boil and blanch the *la mian* sticks for 2 minutes until soft. Drain and plunge immediately into a basin of cold water. Refrigerate the *la mian* until cold.

Bring the ingredients for the beef consommé to the boil in a pot, then lower the heat and simmer, uncovered, for 2 hours until the consommé is reduced to 1 litre (32 fl oz / 4 cups) and the beef is tender. Add the seasoning and stir to mix well. Remove the beef and set it aside. Strain the consommé.

Cut the beef into 4 portions.

Heat 100 ml (3¹⁄₃ fl oz) of the strained consommé in a small pot. Add the sliced beef and thicken the consommé with ¹⁄₂ tsp of cornflour, mixed first with 1 tsp water. This will glaze the beef.

Divide the *la mian* into 4 portions. Place an 8-cm (3-in) wide ring cutter in an individual serving bowl. Fill the ring with *la mian* and press down lightly to compress the noodles, then remove the ring cutter. Repeat this procedure to make 3 more servings.

Sprinkle the *la mian* with seaweed powder. Top with a slice of glazed beef and ladle some beef consommé around the *la mian*. Serve immediately.

WARM GLUTINOUS RICE
WITH SEARED FOIE GRAS

SERVES 4

Glutinous rice *200 g (7 oz), soaked overnight*

Cooking oil *2 Tbsp*

Dried prawns (shrimps) *40 g (1½ oz), rinsed and minced*

Shiitake mushrooms *40 g (1½ oz), caps wiped and minced*

Light soy sauce *½ tsp*

Dark soy sauce *¼ tsp*

Oyster sauce *½ tsp*

Sugar *½ tsp*

Sesame oil *¼ tsp*

Ground white pepper *⅛ tsp*

Foie gras *4, each about 40 g (1½ oz)*

Salt *⅛ tsp*

Cornflour (cornstarch) *1 tsp*

Salted egg yolk *1*

Baby bok choy *4, blanched*

Garnish
Chopped chives

Drain the soaked glutinous rice and place into a steaming container. Steam the rice for 30–40 minutes, or until the rice is tender but still firm to the bite.

Heat 1 Tbsp oil in a wok and sauté the minced dried prawns until fragrant and golden brown. Add the steamed glutinous rice and mushrooms. Season with the light and dark soy sauces, oyster sauce, sugar, sesame oil and pepper. Divide the rice into 4 portions.

Coat the inside of a 4-cm (1.5-in) ring cutter with oil. Spoon a portion of the rice into the ring and press the rice down to compact it. Remove the ring and repeat this step to make 4 servings in total. Steam the rice for another 1 minute, then arrange on serving plates.

Rub the foie gras with salt and sprinkle with cornflour. Heat the remaining 1 Tbsp oil in a pan and sear the foie gras until lightly browned on both sides. Place the seared foie gras on the rice. Garnish with chives.

Coat the salted egg yolk with oil. Using the flat side of a cleaver, smash the egg yolk into a thin sheet. Peel off 4 small pieces of egg yolk and steam them for about 20 seconds.

Serve the rice and foie gras with salted egg yolk and baby bok choy on the side. Garnish with chives if desired.

FRIED RICE WITH CRABMEAT, DRIED SCALLOPS, EGG WHITE AND BRAISED WHOLE ABALONE

SERVES 6

Cooking oil *4 Tbsp*

Egg whites *4, beaten*

Steamed white rice *600 g (1 lb 5¹/₃ oz), refrigerated overnight*

Prepared dried scallops *(see p148) 80 g (3 oz), shredded*

Thai asparagus *30 g (1 oz), blanched and cut into small cubes*

Carrot *30 g (1 oz), peeled, blanched and cut into small cubes*

Salt *1 tsp*

Sugar *¹/₂ tsp*

Ground white pepper *¹/₄ tsp*

Cornflour (cornstarch) *³/₄ tsp*

Chinese cooking wine (*hua tiao*)

Braised Abalone

Canned abalones *1 can (6 in a can)*

Canned abalone juice

Chicken *500 g (1 lb 1¹/₂ oz), cut into cubes and parboiled*

Lean pork *500 g (1 lb 1¹/₂ oz), cut into cubes and parboiled*

Chicken feet *100 g (3¹/₂ oz), poached*

Water *3 litres (96 fl oz / 12 cups)*

Rock sugar *40 g (1¹/₂ oz)*

Dark soy sauce *¹/₄ tsp*

Spring onion (scallion) *1*

Ginger *2 slices*

Heat the oil in a wok and add the egg whites. Stir, then add the rice and cook lightly. Add the prepared scallops, asparagus, carrot, salt, sugar and pepper. Stir-fry to mix well and cook until the rice is fragrant.

Divide the rice into 6 portions. Place a 5-cm (2-in) wide ring cutter in a deep serving plate or bowl, and spoon 1 portion of the rice into the ring. Press the rice down so it takes the shape of ring cutter. Repeat this step to make 6 servings in total.

Combine the ingredients for the braised abalone in a pot and simmer, uncovered, for 3 hours. After simmering, place the pot in a steamer and steam for 1 hour. Remove the abalones and strain the stock.

Heat ¹/₂ Tbsp of oil in a wok and add one-third of the strained stock and the abalones. Taste the stock and add salt if necessary. Stir some dark soy sauce into the stock for colour, if preferred. Stir in ¹/₄ tsp of cornflour to thicken mixture, then place an abalone on top of each mound of rice.

Reheat the remaining stock and add the cooking wine. Thicken with ¹/₂ tsp of cornflour, mixed first with 1 tsp water. Ladle this stock around the rice and serve hot.

CHILLED PEAR WITH RED AND WHITE WINE

SERVES 4

Red Wine Pears
Pears (Nashi or Anjou) *4*
Water *1 litre (32 fl oz / 4 cups)*
Red wine *300 ml (10 fl oz / 1¼ cups)*
Blackcurrant syrup *200 ml (6½ fl oz)*
Cinnamon stick *1*
Star anise *2*
Raisins *50 g (2 oz)*
Chinese wolfberries *50 g (2 oz)*

White Wine Pears
Pears (Nashi or Anjou) *4*
Water *1 litre (32 fl oz / 4 cups)*
White wine *300 ml (10 fl oz / 1¼ cups)*
Vodka *4 Tbsp*
Rock sugar *100 g (3½ oz)*
Bay leaves *2*
Lemon *½*
Salted plums *2*

Garnish
Honey
Osmanthus blossoms

Pare the pears. Leave the stalks in place. Bring the remaining ingredients for the red wine pears to the boil in a pot, then add the pears. Lower the heat and simmer the pears for 35 minutes, or until the pears are soft but still hold their shape.

Strain the marinade into a bowl and place the pears back into the marinade. Cover and refrigerate until the pears are cold.

Repeat the steps above to prepare the white wine pears.

Serve the pears cold, drizzled with honey and garnished with osmanthus blossoms.

NOTE These pears can be prepared in advance and kept refrigerated in the marinade for up to 1 week.

WARM CHOCOLATE SOUFFLÉ WITH BERRIES AND VANILLA ICE CREAM

SERVES 10

Chocolate Soufflé

Dark chocolate (minimum 50% cocoa) *225 g (8 oz), chopped*

Unsalted butter *170 g (6 oz)*

Sugar *280 g (10 oz)*

Cornflour (cornstarch) *25 g (1 oz)*

Egg yolks *4*

Eggs *4*

Toppings (Optional)

Raspberries *10*

Blackcurrants *10*

Cape gooseberries *10*

Vanilla ice cream *4 large scoops*

Mint leaves *10 sprigs*

Cocoa powder *for dusting*

Icing (confectioner's) sugar *for dusting*

Combine the ingredients for the chocolate soufflé in a small mixing bowl and refrigerate the mixture overnight. (This mixture can be kept refrigerated for up to 1 week. Simply remove the mixture from the refrigerator and bake whenever you need a quick dessert.)

Prepare 10 soufflé moulds, each about 8 cm (3 in) in diameter. Grease the inside of the moulds with unsalted butter and dust with plain flour. Half-fill the moulds with the chilled batter, then place them in a preheated fan-assisted oven at 190°C (370°F) for 8–12 minutes, until the soufflés have risen.

Turn the soufflés over onto serving plates and serve with assorted fruit and vanilla ice cream if desired. Dust the soufflés with cocoa powder and icing sugar.

NOTE Oven temperatures vary, so bake one soufflé first to ensure that the oven temperature is correct. You may need to try this recipe out several times before you perfect it.

YELLOW PUMPKIN CUSTARD

SERVES 8

Yellow pumpkin *1, about 500 g*
  (1 lb 1¹/₂ oz)

Eggs *4*

Milk *250 ml (8 fl oz / 1 cup)*

Vanilla essence *¹/₂ tsp*

Sugar *180 g (6¹/₂ oz)*

Raspberry Sauce

Red capsicum *1, small, about 20 g*
  (²/₃ oz)

Raspberries *50 g (2 oz)*

Water *4 Tbsp*

Garnish (Optional)

Roasted walnuts *8*

Mint leaves *8 sprigs*

Prepare this dessert a day ahead.

Prepare the raspberry sauce. Char-grill the capsicum until the skin is black and charred. Soak the capsicum in cold water for a few minutes, then peel off the skin. Cut the capsicum in half and remove the seeds. Blend (process) the capsicum with the raspberries and water to get a smooth purée. Refrigerate the sauce until it is cold.

Cut the cap off the pumpkin, Using a spoon, scrape out and discard the seeds.

Beat the eggs, milk, vanilla essence and sugar until the mixture is pale in colour, then pour it into the prepared pumpkin. Place the pumpkin into the steamer and steam it for 45–60 minutes, or until the custard is set.

Leave the pumpkin and custard to cool before refrigerating it overnight. Cut the pumpkin into 8 wedges and serve with the raspberry sauce. Garnish with walnuts and mint leaves if desired.

Mango Purée

Mango *1, peeled and seeded*

Whipping cream *3 tsp*

Sugar syrup* *3 tsp*

Yam Paste

Yam (taro) *200 g (7 oz)*

Sugar *50 g (2 oz)*

Plain (all-purpose) flour *¼ tsp*

Whipping cream *3 Tbsp*

Fried Dough Balls

Dim sum flour *100 g (3½ oz)*

Cornflour (cornstarch) *¼ tsp*

Plain (all-purpose) flour *¼ tsp*

Water *3 Tbsp*

White sesame seeds *¼ tsp*

Black sesame seeds *¼ tsp*

Cooking oil *for deep-frying*

Garnish

Blackcurrants

Mint leaves

MODERN TEOCHEW YAM PASTE

Combine the ingredients for the mango purée in a blender (food processor) and blend into a smooth purée. Refrigerate the purée until it is cold.

Prepare the yam paste. Peel the yam and cut it into small pieces. Steam the yam for about 30 minutes, or until it is soft. Place the steamed yam into a blender with the remaining ingredients and blend until the mixture is smooth. Refrigerate the paste until it is cold.

Prepare the fried dough balls. Combine all the ingredients, except the sesame seeds and oil, and knead lightly into a dough. Roll the dough into a cylinder about 2.5 cm (1 in) in diameter. Cut the dough into 4 pieces, then roll each piece into a ball. Coat the balls with the white and black sesame seeds.

Heat the oil for deep-frying, then deep-fry the balls over very low heat. As the balls cook, they will float. Hold them down using a ladle, so they are completely covered with oil and will cook more thoroughly. Do this constantly for about 20 minutes until the balls have expanded to about 3 times their original size.

Spoon the chilled mango purée into small shot glasses. Add some yam paste on top and garnish with blackcurrants and mint leaves. Place the fried dough balls on top and serve immediately. The fried dough balls will deflate in about 10 minutes as they cool.

NOTE The texture and quality of yam differs from yam to yam. Unfortunately, the quality of the yam will only be revealed after steaming it. If the steamed yam is watery, discard it and start over. This type of yam is not suitable for use in this recipe.

*SUGAR SYRUP

Sugar *300 g (11 oz)*

Water *150 ml (5 fl oz)*

Combine the sugar and water in a pot and bring to the boil over low heat, stirring, for about 15 minutes, until the sugar dissolves completely and the syrup is slightly thickened. Leave to cool before storing in the refrigerator. Use as needed.

HOMEMADE LYCHEE SHERBET

Sherbet

Lychees *300 g (11 oz), use canned lychees if fresh ones are not available*

Fresh milk *100 ml (3¹/₃ fl oz)*

Honey *4 Tbsp*

Yuzu juice *4 Tbsp*

Garnish

Lychee

Finely grated green lime zest

Prepare this dessert a day ahead.

Combine the ingredients for the sherbet in a blender (food processor) and blend into a purée. Place the purée into a freezer container and freeze it overnight.

Scrape the sherbet using a metal spoon when it is ready for serving. Garnish with lychee and lime zest.

SERVES 4

STUFFED RED DATE

Large dried red dates *16*

Fine glutinous rice flour *200 g (7 oz)*

Cold water *2 Tbsp*

Cooking oil *for deep-frying*

Syrup

Small dried red dates *100 g (3¹/₂ oz), rinsed*

Osmanthus blossoms *20 g (²/₃ oz)*

Water *300 ml (10 fl oz / 1¹/₄ cups)*

Sugar *200 g (7 oz)*

Honey *100 ml (3¹/₂ fl oz)*

Salted plums *3*

Sake *4 Tbsp*

Garnish

Osmanthus blossoms

Make a cut along the length of the large red dates and remove the seed.

Combine the glutinous rice flour and cold water and knead the mixture into a dough. Stuff a small amount of this dough into each large red date.

Bring a pot of water to the boil. This will be for boiling the red dates after deep-frying them.

Heat the oil for deep-frying over low heat and deep-fry the stuffed red dates for about 1 minute. The dough should remain soft and not become crisp. Drain the dates well, then place them in boiling water for about 1 minute. Drain well.

Combine the ingredients for the syrup in a small pot and simmer until the syrup is reduced and thick. This takes about 30 minutes. Strain the syrup into a bowl and add the stuffed red dates. Mix well. Serve the red dates garnished with osmanthus blossoms.

COCONUT ICE CREAM
ON YELLOW PUMPKIN PURÉE

SERVES 4

Store-bought coconut ice cream
  4 large scoops

Yellow Pumpkin Purée
Yellow pumpkin *200 g (7 oz)*
Water *4 Tbsp*
Coconut milk *2 Tbsp*
Whipping cream *2 Tbsp*
Sugar *35 g (1 oz)*

Garnish
Skinned grated coconut *2 Tbsp*
Sterculia seed (*pang da hai*) *1*
Mint leaves *4 sprigs*

Prepare the pumpkin purée. Peel the pumpkin and cut it in half. Remove the seeds and cut the flesh into small pieces.

Steam the pumpkin for 20 minutes, then place the pumpkin into a blender (food processor) and purée it together with the remaining ingredients until a smooth purée is achieved. Refrigerate the purée until cold.

Spread the grated coconut out on a baking tray and bake in a preheated oven at 180°C (350°F) for 20 minutes, or until lightly browned. Remove the tray from the oven every 5 minutes to toss the coconut around to ensure even browning.

Soak the sterculia seed for about 20 minutes to allow the jelly inside the seed to expand. Remove all traces of skin from the jelly.

Serve the pumpkin purée, topped with ice cream and jelly from the sterculia seed. Garnish with toasted grated coconut and mint leaves.

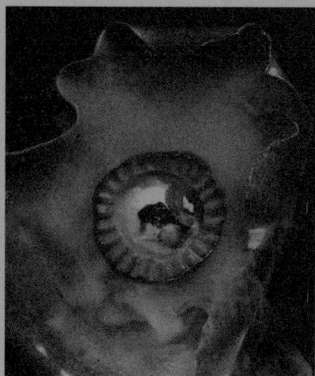

YELLOW PUMPKIN PURÉE WITH MANGO, WARM GLUTINOUS RICE AND COCONUT ICE CREAM

SERVES 4

Whole yellow pumpkins *4, small, each about 350 g (12 oz)*

Black glutinous rice *40 g (1¹/₂ oz), soaked overnight*

Mango *1, about 120 g (4¹/₂ oz), peeled, seeded and diced*

Store-bought coconut ice cream
4 large scoops

Pumpkin Purée
Yellow pumpkin *200 g (7 oz)*

Water *4 Tbsp*

Fresh coconut milk *2 Tbsp*

Whipping cream *2 Tbsp*

Sugar *35 g (1¹/₄ oz)*

Garnish
Chopped, unsalted pistachio nuts

Mint leaves

Dry ice (optional)

Prepare the whole pumpkins. Cut the tops off the pumpkins and scrape out the seeds. Steam the pumpkins for about 20 minutes, or until they are soft. Leave the pumpkins to cool to room temperature, then refrigerate them until cold.

Prepare the pumpkin purée. Peel the pumpkin and cut it in half. Remove the seeds and cut the flesh into smaller pieces. Steam the flesh for about 20 minutes, then purée the flesh together with the remaining ingredients until a smooth purée is achieved. Refrigerate the purée until cold.

Drain the black glutinous rice and place it in a small pot with 300 ml (10 fl oz / 1¹/₄ cups) water. Simmer, uncovered, for about 30 minutes, or until almost all the water has evaporated and the rice moist and tender. Add more water as necessary while the rice is simmering. Set the rice aside.

Spoon the diced mango into the chilled whole pumpkins and ladle some pumpkin purée over. Top with glutinous rice and ice cream. Garnish with pistachio and mint leaves. Serve in a large bowl of dry ice, if desired.

Weights and Measures

Quantities for this book are given in Metric, Imperial and American (spoon) measures. Standard spoon and cup measurements used are: 1 tsp = 5 ml, 1 Tbsp = 15 ml, 1 cup = 250 ml. All measures are level unless otherwise stated.

LIQUID AND VOLUME MEASURES

Metric	Imperial	American
5 ml	$1/6$ fl oz	1 teaspoon
10 ml	$1/3$ fl oz	1 dessertspoon
15 ml	$1/2$ fl oz	1 tablespoon
60 ml	2 fl oz	$1/4$ cup (4 tablespoons)
85 ml	$2 1/2$ fl oz	$1/3$ cup
90 ml	3 fl oz	$3/8$ cup (6 tablespoons)
125 ml	4 fl oz	$1/2$ cup
180 ml	6 fl oz	$3/4$ cup
250 ml	8 fl oz	1 cup
300 ml	10 fl oz ($1/2$ pint)	$1 1/4$ cups
375 ml	12 fl oz	$1 1/2$ cups
435 ml	14 fl oz	$1 3/4$ cups
500 ml	16 fl oz	2 cups
625 ml	20 fl oz (1 pint)	$2 1/2$ cups
750 ml	24 fl oz ($1 1/5$ pints)	3 cups
1 litre	32 fl oz ($1 3/5$ pints)	4 cups
1.25 litres	40 fl oz (2 pints)	5 cups
1.5 litres	48 fl oz ($2 2/5$ pints)	6 cups
2.5 litres	80 fl oz (4 pints)	10 cups

DRY MEASURES

Metric	Imperial
30 grams	1 ounce
45 grams	$1 1/2$ ounces
55 grams	2 ounces
70 grams	$2 1/2$ ounces
85 grams	3 ounces
100 grams	$3 1/2$ ounces
110 grams	4 ounces
125 grams	$4 1/2$ ounces
140 grams	5 ounces
280 grams	10 ounces
450 grams	16 ounces (1 pound)
500 grams	1 pound, $1 1/2$ ounces
700 grams	$1 1/2$ pounds
800 grams	$1 3/4$ pounds
1 kilogram	2 pounds, 3 ounces
1.5 kilograms	3 pounds, $4 1/2$ ounces
2 kilograms	4 pounds, 6 ounces

OVEN TEMPERATURE

	°C	°F	Gas Regulo
Very slow	120	250	1
Slow	150	300	2
Moderately slow	160	325	3
Moderate	180	350	4
Moderately hot	190/200	370/400	5/6
Hot	210/220	410/440	6/7
Very hot	230	450	8
Super hot	250/290	475/550	9/10

LENGTH

Metric	Imperial
0.5 cm	$1/4$ inch
1 cm	$1/2$ inch
1.5 cm	$3/4$ inch
2.5 cm	1 inch